STECK·VAUGHN

ENGLISH ESSENTIALS

A REFRESHER COURSE

By Jewel Varnado

Consultants:
Frank Capurso
Elaine Shelton

Steck-Vaughn Adult Education Advisory Council

Donna Amstutz
Asst. Project Director
Northern Area Adult Education Service Center
Northern Illinois University
DeKalb, Illinois

Sharon Darling
President, National Center for Family Literacy
Louisville, Kentucky

Roberta Pittman
Director, Project C3 Adult Basic Education
Detroit Public Schools
Detroit, Michigan

Elaine Shelton
President, Shelton Associates
Consultant, Competency-Based Adult Education
Austin, Texas

STECK·VAUGHN
COMPANY

About the Author

Jewel Varnado earned her bachelor's and master's degrees in educational psychology and her Ph.D. in adult education from Florida State University. She received the Florida Adult Education Association's Outstanding Service Award and successfully served as an instructor and a supervisor of adult education in Florida. She also is the author of other books for adult education, including *Basic Science for Living*, a two-book series, and *Learning Our Language*.

ISBN 0–8114–4694–8

Copyright © 1991 Steck-Vaughn Company.

6 7 8 9 0 DBH 96 95

CONTENTS

The following pretest will help you to discover your strengths and weaknesses in grammar and usage. After you have completed the test, refer to the answer key at the back of the book to find the correct answers. The chart on page 7 will indicate the pages in the book that will require special concentration if specific items are answered incorrectly.

Choose the correct items for each. Blacken the numbers to the right that correspond to your choices.

1. A complete sentence has a (phrase, subject) and a
   1   2
   (predicate, clause) and makes sense by itself.   ① ② ③ ④
   3   4
2. An adverb clause at the beginning of a sentence is followed
   by a (comma, semicolon). A (comma, semicolon) comes
   1   2   3   4
   before the conjunction that joins two independent clauses in
   a compound sentence.   ① ② ③ ④
3. A (comma, semicolon) is used between two independent
   1   2
   clauses if there is no conjunction between them.
   At the end of an interrogative sentence
   a (question mark, exclamation point) is added.   ① ② ③ ④
   3   4

Choose the proper end punctuation for the following two sentences:

4. The sign says that smoking is not allowed in the building
   (period, question mark)
   1   2
   Where is the fire exit (period, question mark)   ① ② ③ ④
                          3   4
5. A (comma, semicolon) comes before a conjunctive adverb.
   1   2
   A (comma, semicolon) follows a conjunctive adverb.   ① ② ③ ④
   3   4

Choose the correct items for each. Blacken the numbers to the right that correspond to your choices.

6. A complex sentence contains one (independent, dependent)
   1   2
   clause and one or more (independent, dependent) clauses. ① ② ③ ④
   3   4
7. The U.S. (Constitution, constitution) is an important
   1   2
   (document, Document) that was written in Philadelphia.   ① ② ③ ④
   3   4
8. This (oriental, Oriental) vase was made in (China, china). ① ② ③ ④
   1   2   3   4
9. Quotation marks are used to set off (direct quotations,
   1
   indirect quotations) and (slang words, proper nouns).   ① ② ③ ④
   2   3   4

10. You told me the (street, Street) we were looking for was
    ¹ ²
    Pine (street, Street).
    ³ ⁴   ① ② ③ ④

11. We moved to the (south, South) from the (Midwest,
    ¹ ² ³
    midwest).
    ⁴   ① ② ③ ④

12. (Only the first word, The first word and all the nouns) in
    ¹ ²
    the (salutation, closing phrase) of a letter should be
    ³ ⁴
    capitalized.   ① ② ③ ④

13. A colon is used when a (series, verb) is introduced and
    ¹ ²
    after the (salutation, closing) of a letter.
    ³ ⁴   ① ② ③ ④

14. A dash is used to indicate a sudden change or break in
    (the subject, thought, the salutation of a letter, the verb).
    ¹ ² ³ ⁴   ① ② ③ ④

15. Commas are used to separate words in a (phrase, series),
    ¹ ²
    and they are also used to separate the name of a town
    from the name of a (month, state).
    ³ ⁴   ① ② ③ ④

16. I can hear the three (babys, babies) (crying, cring) in the
    ¹ ² ³ ⁴
    nursery.   ① ② ③ ④

17. There are six (deer, deers) eating the peelings from
    ¹ ²
    (potatos, potatoes).
    ³ ⁴   ① ② ③ ④

18. The team (is, are) taking a plane; the group of coaches
    ¹ ²
    (is, are) visiting with various members.
    ³ ⁴   ① ② ③ ④

19. We will meet at (Jane and Bill's, Jane's and Bill's)
    ¹ ²
    house, and then we will drop by (Carla's and Sam's,
    ³
    Carla and Sam's) apartments.
    ⁴   ① ② ③ ④

20. That (woman's, womans') briefcase is in the
    ¹ ²
    (Garcia's, Garcias') car.
    ³ ⁴   ① ② ③ ④

21. It was (she, her) who told (him, he) about the fire.
    ¹ ² ³ ⁴   ① ② ③ ④

22. Jill will be the one (whom, who) will make the
    ¹ ²
    announcement to (whoever, whomever) is in the room.
    ³ ⁴   ① ② ③ ④

23. Choose the underlined words that are demonstrative
    pronouns:
    <u>Who</u>, <u>That</u>, <u>Which</u>, <u>Those</u>.
    ¹ ² ³ ⁴   ① ② ③ ④

24. He (sought, seeked) to find his dog who (dove, dived) into
    ¹ ² ³ ⁴
    the water.   ① ② ③ ④

25. (Its, It's) time to leave for the movie if you (dont, don't)
    ¹ ² ³ ⁴
    want to be late.   ① ② ③ ④

26. An (adverb, adjective) modifies a (noun, verb). ① ② ③ ④
    1   2   3   4

27. Which do you like (best, better), chocolate or vanilla?
              1   2
    Of chocolate, vanilla, and strawberry, which do you like
    (more, most)? ① ② ③ ④
      3   4

28. Choose the underlined words that are prepositions: At the
                                                       1
    corner of the block is an old drug store. ① ② ③ ④
           2   3   4

29. Choose the underlined words that are coordinate conjunc-
    tions: The car and the truck had a wreck, but no one
                  1   2   3
    was injured. ① ② ③ ④
    4

30. Choose the underlined words that are interjections: Help!,
                                                          1
    No, Yes, Wow!. ① ② ③ ④
    2   3   4

31. Choose the underlined words that are subordinate conjunc-
    tions: and, when, never, although. ① ② ③ ④
           1   2   3   4

32. Do you (expect, suppose) that her feelings are very
              1   2
    (different from, different than) yours? ① ② ③ ④
         3   4

33. Words that mean the opposite are called (antonyms,
                                              1
    synonyms); the word that means the same as *alter* is
    2
    (retain, change). ① ② ③ ④
      3   4

34. The dump (cite, site) was (too, to) close to the highway. ① ② ③ ④
              1   2   3   4

35. The spelling of that word looked (weird, wierd) to Jim so
                                       1   2
    he (siezed, seized) the opportunity to change it. ① ② ③ ④
        3   4

Pretest Correlation Chart

If you make a mistake on any items in the Pretest, use this chart to find the page where a review on that subject can be found. An asterisk (*) separates review pages that are correlated to two-part test items that measure more than one content area.

Pretest Item #	Review Pages	Pretest Item #	Review Pages	Pretest Item #	Review Pages	Pretest Item #	Review Pages
1	8–11	10	88–92	18	30–31	27	68–69
2	78–79	11	88–92	19	40–41	28	72–73
3	82 * 9–10, 77	12	89	20	40–41	29	73–74
4	9–10, 77	13	82–83	21	50–53	30	74
5	78–79, 82	14	83	22	55–56	31	73–74
6	15–17	15	81	23	57–58	32	99–100
7	88–92	16	37–39, 112–113	24	26–29	33	109
8	88–92		* 112–113	25	32–33	34	110
9	84–86	17	37–39	26	65–67	35	111

Using Sentences

Lesson 1 The Sentence

A sentence is a group of words that expresses a complete thought. A sentence makes sense by itself. A sentence also contains a subject and a predicate.

Complete Sentence	Incomplete Sentence
The firefighter scaled the ladder.	Firefighter scaled.
We went to the meeting.	Going to the meeting on Friday.
That car passed us before.	Down the street.
Show him the door.	Called.
What is that?	A piston.

- **The subject names a person, place, or thing about which we are talking or writing.**
- **The predicate tells something that the subject is or does.**

   Look at the complete sentences above. The subject of the first sentence is *firefighter*. The predicate of the sentence is *scaled*. Find the subject and the predicate of each of the other sentences. (The subject of the fourth sentence is not expressed. In sentences of this kind, *you* is always understood to be the subject.)

Practice 1

Write **S** before each complete sentence. If the group of words is not a complete sentence, write **F** (for "sentence fragment") in the blank. Add a period (.), a question mark (?), or an exclamation point (!) at the end of each complete sentence. Then make each fragment into a complete sentence by adding needed words and punctuation.

1. _____ The car being fixed at the garage today

2. _____ Have you met Mr. Moore

3. _____ Please give me the tack hammer

4. _____ No, that way

5. _____ Across the street and down about two blocks

6. _____ The personnel manager gave me an application blank to fill out

7. _____ Good mechanics are usually well paid for their work

8. _____ Where is my new shirt

9. _____ Hey, Bill, I got a raise today

10. _____ When we go to the supermarket for our groceries

11. _____ Empty the ice bag here

12. _____ That was an interesting story about Joe Lopez in Sunday's paper

13. _____ When will you be ready to take the driving test

14. _____ Sometime next week

15. _____ Fifty dollars is a ridiculous price for that dress

16. _____ How long have you been working at the machine shop

17. _____ I bought a good-looking shirt at the half-price sale

18. _____ Let's take the kids on a picnic next Saturday

19. _____ And a pretty new chair in the corner

Writing Sentences Correctly

Remember these rules for writing sentences correctly:

■ **Begin each sentence with a capital letter.**

■ **Place a period at the end of a sentence that makes a statement, a request, or a command.**
We fished for several hours at the lake. (statement)
Please close the door. (request)
Face the front of the bus. (command)

■ **Place a question mark at the end of a sentence that asks a question.**
What is the name of that book?
Have you planned your fishing trip?

■ **Place an exclamation point at the end of a sentence that expresses strong feeling or emotion.**
Stop running in front of cars! You might be killed!

■ **Do not run together sentences with *and* or *and then*.**

POOR: We met at the park and we went swimming and then we had a picnic and later we went home.

BETTER: We met at the park. After swimming, we had a picnic. Later we went home.

Practice 2

Each numbered group of words below contains two or three sentences run together. Decide where each sentence should end. Begin each new sentence with a capital letter. Place the correct mark of punctuation—a period, a question mark, or an exclamation point—at the end of each sentence. The first one is done for you.

1. Have you been fishing this year? ^Mmy friend and I went fishing last week-end. ^Wwe fished on my friend's ranch.

2. The efficiency of a machine is always less than 100 percent perhaps you can explain why

3. Who made the first wheel we do not know the first wheels were probably square time brought about changes and improvements

4. Did you hear the news we will have to wait an hour for the doctor

5. A ship loaded with cargo was anchored in the harbor suddenly we heard a loud explosion almost immediately smoke began to rise from the stern

6. What a wonderful magician she is have you seen her act she has been on television

7. We caught the bus at 8:15 it always seems to be late

8. Don't be upset I'll help you paint the room in the morning

9. I went to the market and purchased some fish then I took them home and cooked them

10. Take the package to the office and give it to Mrs. Stanton then come back here quickly

11. Always shop here you can buy things at a lower price

Learning More About Subjects and Predicates

Either the subject or the predicate of a sentence may consist of one word or a group of words. In the following sentences the subject is underlined once. The predicate is underlined twice.

The first lessons taught him how to change the car's oil.
First Federal Savings and Loan has just declared a dividend.

Other Rules About Sentences

- The **simple subject** is usually a noun (name of a person, place, or thing) or a pronoun (words such as *he, she, they, it,* etc., which take the place of a noun or nouns). The simple subject might also be a word that names an action. (*Swimming* is good exercise.) A word ending in *-ing* is not used as a verb unless it has a helping verb before it.
- A **compound subject** consists of two or more subjects (joined by *and* or *or*) used with the same predicate.
- The **simple predicate** is a verb (one word) or a verb phrase (two or more words).
- A **compound predicate** consists of two or more verbs (joined by *and* or *or*) used with the same subject.
- The word *not* or the contraction *n't* is not a part of the verb.
- The subject usually comes before the verb, but sometimes it follows the verb or comes between parts of a verb phrase.
- The words *there* or *here* are never used as the subject of a sentence.

Practice 3

Make sentences by adding a subject to each of the first eight sentences and by adding a predicate to each of the last three sentences.

1. _____ bought a new boat last Tuesday.

2. _____ is a good place to shop for fresh vegetables.

3. When will _____ finish the cabinet?

4. There are many _____ in the new shopping center.

5. The first _____ of winter occurs in December.

6. _____ and _____ will make the sandwiches for the picnic.

7. Here is the _____ from the doctor.

8. Many wild, fierce, large _____ roamed in the jungle.

9. The Matthews Company _____.

10. Our children _____ and _____.

11. _____ you _____?

Lesson II Two Kinds of Sentences

Simple sentences have only one subject and one predicate (either or both of which may be compound). All sentences used in the practice material in Lesson I are simple sentences. In Lesson II you will be working with **compound sentences**.

Rules for Joining Independent Clauses

A compound sentence is really two or more simple sentences (called independent clauses) joined together by a conjunction, a conjunctive adverb, or a semicolon.

- **When the conjunctions *and, but, or, for,* or *nor* are used to join two independent clauses, they are preceded by a comma unless the clauses are very short.**

  Bring sandwiches, and I will supply the coffee.
  We must leave early, for we should arrive before noon.

- **When the conjunctive adverbs *therefore, however, moreover, yet, so, indeed, accordingly, besides, hence, then, thus, nevertheless, still, also, consequently,* and *otherwise* are used to join two independent clauses, the conjunctive adverbs are usually preceded by a semicolon and followed by a comma.**

  A strange sound reached our ears; however, it was very indistinct.

- **In sentences that contain two independent clauses, if either independent clause contains a comma or commas, the conjunction may be preceded by a semicolon.**

  Days, weeks, and months passed; but Grandfather waited patiently.

- **If no conjunction or conjunctive adverb is used between independent clauses, the clauses are separated by a semicolon.**

  Samuel works hard; he will succeed.

Practice 1

Underline each subject once and each predicate twice. Remember that each clause will have a subject and a predicate. Circle the conjunction, conjunctive adverb, or semicolon between clauses.

1. The rain had stopped, and we could see a rainbow in the distance.
2. We must call the ranger at once, or he won't be able to photograph the bear.
3. She passed the test easily, but many more tests lay ahead.
4. De Soto searched for gold; however, he found the villages of the Pueblo people.

5. The boy would listen to no one, nor would he think for himself.
6. The native performers sang songs of joy; consequently, the hours seemed shorter.
7. The man grumbled, and then he walked away.
8. Mice have been used for experiments, and many people don't like the idea.

Practice 2

Add a conjunction to each sentence. Punctuate the sentences correctly.

1. Susan filled out the credit form _____ she was given a checking account.

2. Movies seen on the late show are old _____ many are very good.

3. She must fill out an application blank _____ she will not be considered for the job.

4. I have the work completed _____ it is well done.

5. Jon will not ask for help _____ he will not accept it when offered.

6. Please write your suggestions for solving the problem _____ I will consider them.

7. The directions were poorly written _____ I still was able to assemble the clock.

8. He could not stand the pressure _____ he quit his job.

9. Wave after wave fell on the beachhead _____ the soldiers held their ground.

10. The machine was broken _____ we were able to repair it in less than an hour.

11. Do you have the reports _____ did you fail to bring them?

12. The band played beautifully _____ no one was dancing.

13. You may laugh _____ I'm convinced I'm correct.

14. You must register by ten o'clock _____ you will be refused admittance.

Practice 3

Add a conjunctive adverb to each sentence and punctuate correctly.

1. You failed to file your income tax on time _____ you will have to pay a penalty.

2. I studied for several hours _____ I did not pass the test.

3. You must be here Friday morning _____ we will cancel the trip.

4. He fell and tore the knee out of his slacks _____ he went home to change.

5. The candidate made a good speech _____ there were few people to hear it.

6. This is a difficult job _____ I will try to do it.

7. Stand still _____ I might stick you with this pin.

8. We cannot get the car fixed _____ we must spend the night here.

Practice 4

The underlined part of each sentence on the left may be correct or incorrect. Select the correct form from the group at the right. Mark the letter of the correct answer in each blank.

1. Native American tribes have lived in America for <u>centuries but</u> some people believe they were originally from Asia.

   ANSWER: _____

   a. Correct as written
   b. centuries; but
   c. centuries, but
   d. centuries. But

2. Flowers, ferns, ribbons, and banners decked the <u>float, and</u> its colors were beautiful.

   ANSWER: _____

   a. Correct as written
   b. float and
   c. float; and
   d. float. And

3. <u>Night fell; and</u> the animals crept away from the village.

   ANSWER: _____

   a. Correct as written
   b. Night fell: and
   c. Night fell. And
   d. Night fell, and

4. Many Irish people went <u>west; however,</u> a large number stayed in New York City.

   ANSWER: _____

   a. Correct as written
   b. west; however;
   c. west, however,
   d. west, however;

5. Put the tools in the <u>cabinet; for</u> we will not use them today.

   ANSWER: _____

   a. Correct as written
   b. cabinet, for,
   c. cabinet, for
   d. cabinet for

Lesson III Complex Sentences

In Lesson III you will be working with the complex sentence. A **complex sentence** contains one independent clause and one or more dependent clauses. A **dependent clause** contains a subject and a predicate, but it does not express a complete thought.

■ **In order to make sense, a dependent clause must be joined to an independent clause.**

Dependent	Independent
when you go to the store	Buy some flour and sugar.
before you leave	Please sign the check.
that we saw	The table has been sold.

The dependent and independent clauses above can be joined in the following ways to form complex sentences. (Notice that a dependent clause can come between parts of an independent clause.)

When you go to the store, buy some flour and sugar.
Buy some flour and sugar when you go to the store.
Before you leave, please sign the check.
Please sign the check before you leave.
The table that we saw has been sold.

■ **A dependent clause is usually joined to an independent clause by using one of the following words (called subordinate conjunctions):**

whenever	what	since	when	until	as
that	where	though	unless	after	which
wherever	in order that	although	while	because	so that
as if	than	if	before	whether	how

Practice 1

Underline each subordinate conjunction. Remember that a subordinate conjunction joins a dependent clause to an independent clause.

1. When the truck is full of gravel, please deliver it to this address.
2. You can put that box wherever you can find an empty spot.
3. This ice will all be melted if we do not get it into a chest quickly.
4. While you are waiting, you may want to read one of these magazines.
5. I stood at the edge of the curb until a car splattered me with water from that puddle.
6. We will not receive the bonus check until the company's books have been audited.

- Dependent clauses that tell *how, when, where, how often,* or *how much* are called **adverbial clauses.** When an adverbial clause is used at the beginning of a sentence, it is separated from the independent clause by a comma. No comma is needed if the adverbial clause follows the independent clause. Look at the first four complex sentences given as examples on page 15. Each contains an adverbial clause. Note the use of commas to set off introductory adverbial clauses.

- Dependent clauses that tell *who, whom, whose, what,* or *which* are called **adjective clauses.** An adjective clause necessary to the meaning of the sentence is a **restrictive clause.** No punctuation is used to set it off. An adjective clause not necessary to the meaning of the sentence is a **nonrestrictive clause.** It is set off by commas. *Who, whom, which,* and *that* introduce adjective clauses.

  Cynthia, who is my neighbor, won the contest. (nonrestrictive)
  The woman who won the contest is my neighbor. (restrictive)
  Tom Rainosek, who was caught speeding, was fined $25. (nonrestrictive)
  Drivers who are caught speeding should be fined. (restrictive)

Practice 2

Underline the independent clause in each sentence. Write **S** over each simple subject and **V** over each verb. Insert commas as needed to set off introductory adverbial clauses and nonrestrictive adjective clauses.

    This leather, which is quite durable, is genuine cowhide.

    When we go to town, we will mail the package.

    Families who live in this block are invited to the party.

1. When Tseng reached for the wrench he tripped.

2. Put this bouquet of yellow roses where everyone can see it.

3. The plants that grew in this garden came from Japan.

4. Although you may not believe it we are really working hard for you.

5. Did you tell Ernesto that I want to see him this morning?

6. Before you go to work please sweep the front porch and the steps.

7. Jane O'Leary who is visiting us sells new cars in Chicago.

8. The city has doubled in size since you moved away ten years ago.

9. Aunt Rebecca who is a minister told us that you were coming here soon.

10. The person who saved the drowning boy was awarded a medal.

11. As I passed the crowd in the park I noticed many small children.

12. Do not leave until the car is repaired.

13. Mr. Jenkins who works at our plant won a prize in the contest.

14. All are to stand while the flag is being raised.

15. The accident which could have been prevented easily caused much damage.

16. Since the utility bill is due today I will pay it at the utility office.

Practice 3

Write sentences by following these instructions.

1. Write a complex sentence that has an introductory adverb clause. _____

_____

2. Write a complex sentence that has an adverb clause after the independent clause.

_____

3. Write a complex sentence that has a restrictive adjective clause between two parts

of an independent clause. _____

_____

4. Write a complex sentence that has a nonrestrictive adjective clause. _____

_____

5. Write a complex sentence that has an introductory adverb clause and an adverb

clause following the independent clause. _____

_____

6. Write a complex sentence that has an adverb clause and an adjective clause.

_____

Directions: Beneath each sentence, you will find four ways of writing the underlined part. Choose the answer that is correct. Blacken the number to the right that corresponds to your choice. If there is no error, mark answer space 4.

1. After the concert <u>ended, we</u> quickly walked to our car.   ① ② ③ ④

    (1) ended; we   (3) ended we
    (2) ended. We   (4) no error

2. The Chengs are our <u>neighbors, however, they</u> are moving
    next month.   ① ② ③ ④

    (1) neighbors, however; they   (3) neighbors; however; they
    (2) neighbors; however, they   (4) no error

3. Our major problem is the lack of <u>money; but</u> we are work-
    ing to solve it.   ① ② ③ ④

    (1) money, but   (3) money. But
    (2) money but   (4) no error

4. After you <u>left; we talked for hours; consequently we</u> were
    too tired to make much sense.   ① ② ③ ④

    (1) left; we talked for hours, consequently, we
    (2) left, we talked for hours; consequently we
    (3) left, we talked for hours; consequently, we
    (4) no error

5. This <u>box which is extremely heavy arrived</u> yesterday.   ① ② ③ ④

    (1) box which is extremely heavy, arrived
    (2) box, which is extremely heavy, arrived
    (3) box; which is extremely heavy; arrived
    (4) no error

6. A hammer, a saw, and some nails must be <u>purchased, and</u>
    then I can start to work.   ① ② ③ ④

    (1) purchased and   (3) purchased; and
    (2) purchased. And   (4) no error

7. The <u>people, who live in this block, are</u> excellent neighbors.   ① ② ③ ④

    (1) people who live in this block are
    (2) people, who live in this block are
    (3) people; who live in this block; are
    (4) no error

8. Mr. Vigil wanted to take a <u>vacation, but</u> he needed to work another week.　　　　　　① ② ③ ④
   (1) vacation. But　　　　　　　(3) vacation but
   (2) vacation; but　　　　　　　(4) no error

9. Our <u>car which was left in the parking lot will</u> need to be washed and waxed.　　　　　① ② ③ ④
   (1) car, which was left in the parking lot, will
   (2) car; which was left in the parking lot; will
   (3) car. Which was left in the parking lot. Will
   (4) no error

10. When Dr. Ramon comes to the <u>office we</u> need to see him immediately.　　　　　　　① ② ③ ④
   (1) Office. We　　　　　　　(3) Office; we
   (2) office, we　　　　　　　(4) no error

11. If your dog can't stay <u>in the yard he'll</u> have to go to the pound.　　　　　　　　① ② ③ ④
   (1) in the yard, he'll　　　　(3) in the yard. He'll
   (2) in the yard; He'll　　　　(4) no error

Write sentences by following these instructions.

12. Write a complex sentence that has an adverbial clause. _____

   _____

   _____

13. Write a complex sentence that has a restrictive adjective clause. _____

   _____

   _____

14. Write a simple sentence. _____

   _____

   _____

Verbs

Lesson I Being Verbs

Being verbs are called linking verbs if they join a subject to a predicate noun, a predicate pronoun, or a predicate adjective, which is an adjective in the predicate that modifies the subject. Some being verbs are listed below:

is	were	has been	can be	will have been
are	am	had been	could be	might have been
was	be	have been	will be	may have been

■ **If the following verbs express a *condition*, they are classified as being verbs. However, some of these words may also be used as action verbs.**

seem	appear	look	feel	sound	turn
become	prove	stand	grow	smell	taste

Study the following examples of the use of a being verb, a being verb of condition, and an action verb.

The youngster's head is hot. (being verb)
The youngster's head feels hot. (being verb—condition)
I felt his hot head. (action)

Practice

Underline each subject once and each being verb twice. There may be more than one subject or verb in a sentence.

1. You appear very sad today.
2. I have been ill for over a week.
3. I am sure that I am your best friend.
4. The work seems difficult, but it is not too hard.
5. All the hotels were large and luxurious.
6. Has the supervisor been helpful to the new employee?

Lesson 11   Action Verbs and Verb Phrases

There are very few being or linking verbs, but many action verbs. Some of the action expressed by these verbs is very noticeable. Such words as *jump, yell, fight,* and *dance* show much action. Other verbs, such as *think, dream, smile,* and *hear,* show very little action. Remember that all verbs except being verbs show action.

Practice 1

Underline each subject once and each action verb twice.

1. I knocked the firecracker from my child's hand.
2. The politician made a good impression on most who listened.
3. At the end of the round, the referee gave the decision.
4. When they announced a five-minute intermission, we went to the lounge.
5. The supervisor posted the new work schedule.
6. The shelter that we found gave us little protection from the rain.
7. With a modest smile, he received the congratulations of his friends.
8. When we reached the beach, Jeanne ran into the water.
9. You must climb this small hill and look toward the east.
10. Steve laughed too much and spoiled the comedian's punch line.
11. Lightning struck the house; flames rose high into the air.
12. Many volunteers assist the regular Red Cross and Salvation Army workers.
13. As a safety precaution, we wore the hard hats all day.

Practice 2

Underline each verb twice. Write **B** over each being verb and **A** over each action verb.

1. Jorge said that the shipment will be late today.

2. My insurance payment should be much lower this year.

3. When you cook this dish, you must be certain that the vegetables are fresh.

4. That painting is colorful, but I would not buy it.

5. This letter is yellow from age, but I will not throw it away.

6. Carmen is very happy, for she got the job that she wanted.

Recognizing Verb Phrases

■ Being verbs can become helping verbs. A verb with a helping verb or verbs is called a verb phrase. A verb phrase is used as a single verb even though the phrase may be composed of two, three, or four words.

| am working | is working | are working |
| had been working | shall be working | will have been working |

■ In some sentences, the verb phrase will be divided into two parts by other words. This division may occur in declarative sentences, but it occurs more often in interrogative sentences.

I will not go with you and Jessie. Can you come with me?
The parents and the children were soon parted. Were they ever lost?

Below is a list of some adverbs that often divide the parts of a verb phrase.

almost	particularly	seldom	too
especially	quite	so	truly
not	rather	somewhat	very
often	really	soon	usually

Practice 3

Underline each verb twice. Be sure to underline both parts of an interrupted verb phrase. Sentences may have more than one verb.

1. I definitely heard you say "You may leave early on Friday."
2. More than three thousand species of snakes are known, but no species is native to Hawaii.
3. As we returned our tools, our names were checked off the list.
4. Tomorrow is the first day of spring, but the weather remains cold.
5. This work has been carelessly done; I will not accept it.
6. In recent years, much oil has been found in Alaska.
7. You cannot expect to find a job when you sit on a park bench every day.
8. We were seeing the Rocky Mountains for the first time; we were speechless.
9. Sandra was a pessimist; she lost hope too quickly.
10. Were you told of his lack of ability and his carelessness?
11. The noisy dancers were ordered off the stage until the director sent for them.
12. This world will be a different place for those who live fifty years from now.
13. You can seldom find two brothers who get along so well.
14. We could hardly hear his voice, but his eyes communicated his thoughts.
15. If the chairperson calls the meeting to order before I return, Sandra will call me.

Lesson III Verb Tense

Tense means "time." The three simple tenses are the present, the past, and the future.

Present Tense	Past Tense	Future Tense
I sing	I sang	I will sing

Understanding Regular Verbs

■ The three principal parts of all verbs are the present, the past, and the past participle. The past tense will usually have a change in form, and the past participle will be used with helping verbs, such as *have, had, has, shall have,* and *will have*. The principal parts of a *regular* verb are easy to learn. The past and the past participle are often alike.

■ The past and the past participle are formed by adding *-d* or *-ed* to regular verbs.

Present:	laugh	dive	walk	stumble
Past:	laughed	dived	walked	stumbled
Past Participle:	laughed	dived	walked	stumbled

■ If a regular one-syllable verb ends in a single consonant preceded by a vowel, the ending consonant must be doubled before *-ed* is added.

Present:	beg	stop	tap	brag
Past:	begged	stopped	tapped	bragged
Past Participle:	begged	stopped	tapped	bragged

■ If regular verbs end in *y* preceded by a consonant, change the *y* to *i* before adding *-ed*.

Present:	carry	study	marry	reply
Past:	carried	studied	married	replied
Past Participle:	carried	studied	married	replied

Understanding Verb Tense

Use the following charts to form and use verb tenses.

Tense	How to Form It	Example
Present	present part of verb (add -s or -es for he, she, or it subjects)	lives
Past	past part of verb	lived
Future	will plus present part	will live
Present perfect	have plus past participle (use has for he, she, or it subjects)	has lived
Past perfect	had plus past participle	had lived
Future perfect	will have plus past participle	will have lived

Tense	When to Use It
Present	(1) When action is happening now (2) With action that usually happens (3) With action that is always true
Past	Action completed before now
Future	Action that will happen later
Present perfect	(1) Action that began in the past and continues to the present (2) Action that happened at an unknown time in the past
Past perfect	Action that happened before another action was completed
Future perfect	Action that did not happen yet, but that will be completed at a specific time in the future

Practice 1

Write the missing parts of these regular verbs.

	Present	Past	Past Participle
1.	help	_____	_____
2.	_____	planned	_____
3.	march	_____	_____
4.	_____	_____	hurried
5.	startle	_____	_____

Present	Past	Past Participle
6. _____	complied	_____
7. _____	omitted	_____
8. _____shop_____	_____	_____
9. _____	ticked	_____
10. _____bar_____	_____	_____
11. _____play_____	_____	_____
12. _____smell_____	_____	_____
13. _____	_____	scurried
14. _____jar_____	_____	_____
15. _____tap_____	_____	_____
16. _____	asked	_____
17. _____	_____	desired
18. _____	replied	_____
19. _____rally_____	_____	_____
20. _____	noticed	_____
21. _____prop_____	_____	_____
22. _____	taped	_____
23. _____ship_____	_____	_____
24. _____	_____	handled
25. _____	moved	_____
26. _____	_____	carried
27. _____brag_____	_____	_____
28. _____	checked	_____
29. _____trap_____	_____	_____
30. _____dive_____	_____	_____
31. _____stare_____	_____	_____
32. _____marry_____	_____	_____

Understanding Irregular Verbs

- The principal parts of *irregular* verbs are not formed by any set rules. They must be learned. Consult your dictionary when you need help.

- Many irregular verbs form the past and the past participle by a change within the word.

Present:	begin	sing	ring
Past:	began	sang	rang
Past Participle:	begun	sung	rung

- The past and the past participle of some irregular verbs are alike.

Present:	buy	sleep	bleed	seek
Past:	bought	slept	bled	sought
Past Participle:	bought	slept	bled	sought

- There are some irregular verbs that make no change in the present, the past, or the past participle.

Present:	burst	hurt	shed	put	set	rid	cut
Past:	burst	hurt	shed	put	set	rid	cut
Past Participle:	burst	hurt	shed	put	set	rid	cut

Principal Parts of Some Troublesome Verbs

Present	Past	Past Participle	Present	Past	Past Participle
am	was	been	climb	climbed	climbed
arise	arose	arisen	clothe	clothed	clothed
attack	attacked	attacked	come	came	come
awake	awoke	awaked (awoken)	creep	crept	crept
			dig	dug	dug
bear	bore	borne	dive	dived	dived
beat	beat	beaten	do	did	done
become	became	become	drag	dragged	dragged
begin	began	begun	draw	drew	drawn
bend	bent	bent	dream	dreamed	dreamed
bite	bit	bitten	drink	drank	drunk
bleed	bled	bled	drive	drove	driven
bless	blessed	blessed	drown	drowned	drowned
blow	blew	blown	dwell	dwelled	dwelled
break	broke	broken	eat	ate	eaten
bring	brought	brought	fight	fought	fought
burn	burned	burned	fly	flew	flown
burst	burst	burst	forget	forgot	forgotten
catch	caught	caught	forgive	forgave	forgiven
choose	chose	chosen	freeze	froze	frozen

Present	Past	Past Participle	Present	Past	Past Participle
get	got	got (gotten)	set	set	set
			sew	sewed	sewed (sewn)
give	gave	given			
go	went	gone	shake	shook	shaken
grow	grew	grown	shine	shone	shone
hang (suspend)	hung	hung	show	showed	showed (shown)
hang (execute)	hanged	hanged	shrink	shrank	shrunk
			sing	sang	sung
hear	heard	heard	sink	sank	sunk
heat	heated	heated	sit	sat	sat
hide	hid	hidden	slay	slew	slain
hold	held	held	sleep	slept	slept
hurt	hurt	hurt	slide	slid	slid
kneel	knelt	knelt	speak	spoke	spoken
know	knew	known	speed	sped	sped
lay	laid	laid	spend	spent	spent
lead	led	led	spit	spat	spat
lend	lent	lent	spring	sprang	sprung
lie (rest)	lay	lain	stand	stood	stood
			steal	stole	stolen
lie (fib)	lied	lied	strike	struck	struck
			swear	swore	sworn
light	lighted (lit)	lighted (lit)	sweep	swept	swept
			swim	swam	swum
lose	lost	lost	swing	swung	swung
mean	meant	meant	take	took	taken
mistake	mistook	mistaken	teach	taught	taught
pay	paid	paid	tear	tore	torn
prove	proved	proved (proven)	throw	threw	thrown
			wake	waked (woke)	waked (woken)
raise	raised	raised			
read	read	read	wear	wore	worn
rid	rid	rid	weave	wove	woven
ride	rode	ridden	weep	wept	wept
ring	rang	rang	wind	wound	wound
rise	rose	risen	wring	wrung	wrung
run	ran	run	write	wrote	written
say	said	said			
see	saw	seen			

Write a sentence using each of the following correctly.

1. past participle of *rise* _____

2. past of *stand* _____

3. past participle of *tear* _____

4. past participle of *rid* _____

5. past of *know* _____

6. past participle of *lose* _____

7. past of *freeze* _____

8. past of *hide* _____

Practice 3

Mark out the incorrect verb. Remember that the past participle form of the verb is used with a helping verb.

1. We have (hid, hidden) the silver in the attic.
2. You have (mistook, mistaken) the intent of the memo sent by the company.
3. The ship had (sank, sunk) in a storm many years ago.
4. I still cannot imagine who has (stole, stolen) the box.
5. Who (hid, hidden) the keys to my car?
6. I (saw, seen) the plans for the new machine we have ordered.
7. The pitcher had (threw, thrown) a fast ball three times in a row.
8. Our neighbor (rang, rung) the doorbell three times.
9. You have always (did, done) an outstanding job since you have worked here.
10. The lion had suddenly (sprang, sprung) on the surprised trainer.
11. Who (threw, throwed) the paper under the sprinkler?
12. The radiator (bursted, burst) when the car became too hot.

Verbs Needing Special Study

Verbs	Meanings	Examples
lie	to stretch out	*Lie* in the shade of the tree. He *lay* down for an hour. No one else has *lain* there.
lay	to place	*Lay* the books side by side. He *laid* the money in my hand. Tom and Mary have *laid* all of the bricks.
set	to place	You may *set* the flowers on the table. *Set* the plants in a row. John has *set* down the package.
rise	to move higher	Do not *rise* until the bell rings. He *rose* and bowed. Carmelita has *risen* early today.
raise	to cause to rise	Did you *raise* the windows? I *raised* three of them. Sue has *raised* the flag.

Troublesome Pairs

Verbs	Meanings	Examples
teach	to show how	I can *teach* you the lesson.
learn	to find out something	She does not *learn* easily.
may	to permit	All of you *may* try to win.
can	to be able	No other mechanic *can* do this.
let	to permit	*Let* us help you.
leave	to go away	I must *leave* now.

Practice 4

Mark out the incorrect verb or verbs in each sentence.

1. (Let, Leave) us go before the thunderstorm gets any worse.
2. Did you say that you had (set, sat) the table?
3. I (can, may) answer that question easily.
4. Yesterday at the beach we (lay, laid) in the sun and relaxed.
5. None of those who had (drank, drunk) the water became ill.
6. Many of the early settlers have (went, gone) away.
7. I can remember nothing that she (learned, taught) me that year.
8. Will you tell the baby to (lie, lay) down?
9. The champion has (swam, swum) in every important competition.
10. That group of men (set, sat) on the store porch each evening.
11. Although I have (ate, eaten) what you prepared, I am still hungry.
12. Have you never (written, wrote) a letter of complaint to the company?
13. Each may (chose, choose) the meeting that he or she will attend.

Lesson IV Subject and Verb Agreement

A verb must agree with its subject in number. A singular subject requires a singular verb, and a plural subject requires a plural verb. Determining whether a subject is singular or plural is sometimes difficult, but subject and verb agreement is only a problem when the present tense of the verb is used.

- **The predicate verb must agree with the subject, not with a noun or a pronoun in a prepositional phrase that separates the subject and the verb.**

    The stack (of wheat cakes) was hot and delicious.
    A trio (of sisters) sings in our choir.

- **Always use the plural verb with the subject *you*.**

    You were late yesterday.

- **The contraction *doesn't* means "does not"; the contraction *don't* means "do not." This fact is often overlooked, and such an incorrect expression as *he don't* is used.**

    He doesn't like the new car. They don't agree at all.

- **The words *there* and *here* can never be subjects. When *there* or *here* is the first word in a sentence, it signals to the reader that the subject will be found elsewhere in the sentence.**

    Here are the six mice. There are the boats in the harbor.

Practice 1

Mark out the incorrect verb.

1. The person running through the streets (is, are) preparing for a big race.
2. They said you (was, were) planning to change jobs in the near future.
3. If you ask me, he (doesn't, don't) look that old.
4. There (is, are) several people standing in line for tickets.
5. Those boxes in my car (is, are) to be stored in the garage.
6. (Was, Were) you planning to send flowers to the funeral?
7. (Doesn't, Don't) you want me to hold your coat while you phone?
8. The dogs in that pen (is, are) very dangerous.

- **A singular verb should be used when the subject is singular.**
    Harold is here now.

- **Use a singular verb when singular compound subjects are joined by *or* or *nor*.**
    Rain or snow is falling over all the states.

30

- **Use a singular verb when the last subject of a singular-plural compound subject, joined by *or* or *nor*, is singular.**

  Either the small oranges or the large apple is for Sarah.

- **Use a singular verb when a singular indefinite pronoun is the subject.**

  Each is in her or his own place. Everybody looks pleased.

- **A singular verb is needed when words that state an amount are used as the subject.**

  Three weeks is a long vacation. Ten dollars is a high price.

- **Use a singular verb with nouns that are singular in meaning but plural in form.**

  Civics is not really difficult.

- **Use a plural verb when the subject is plural.**

  The horses are very wild.

- **Use a plural verb when compound subjects are joined by *and*.**

  You and I are passing this course.

- **Use a plural verb when plural compound subjects are joined by *or* or *nor*.**

  Neither titles nor riches are everlasting.

- **Use a plural verb when the last subject of a singular-plural compound subject, joined by *or* or *nor*, is plural.**

  Neither the general nor the soldiers have arrived.

- **A plural verb is needed when the plural indefinite pronouns *several, few, both,* and *many* are used.**

  Many were present at the dedication.

Practice 2

Singular and plural verbs are given at the beginning of each sentence. Insert the correct verb in each blank.

1. *has, have*   Everybody in this country _____ heard of her.

2. *was, were*   Mr. Daniels, with his two children, _____ in the store.

3. *look, looks*   Each of the children _____ like the Smith family.

4. *need, needs*   Neither the carpenter nor the painters _____ any help.

5. *stand, stands*   A bookcase of old books _____ in the hall.

Lesson V Contractions

Many contractions are the combination of a pronoun and a verb. Do not confuse contractions with possessive forms of words. An apostrophe and -s are used to form the possessive of singular indefinite pronouns. All other pronouns form the plural by a change in the word itself.

Pronoun and Verb Contractions

When the word *it* has an apostrophe and -s, making the word *it's*, the word is not used as a personal pronoun. *It's* then is a contraction for the pronoun *it* and the verb *is*. The *i* in *is* has been omitted, and an apostrophe has been put into the *i's* place.

Possessive Pronouns: its   whose   their   theirs   your

Contractions: it's—it is   who's—who is   they're—they are
there's—there is   you're—you are

Other pronoun and verb contractions include the following:

I've (I have)	we'll (we will)	I'm (I am)	we're (we are)
you'll (you will)	he's (he is)	you've (you have)	she's (she is)
let's (let us)	that's (that is)		

Verb and Adverb Contractions

Another type of contraction combines a verb and an adverb.

don't (do not)	doesn't (does not)	haven't (have not)
there's (there is)	isn't (is not)	hasn't (has not)
aren't (are not)	wasn't (was not)	weren't (were not)
shouldn't (should not)		

Practice 1

Mark out each incorrect word.

1. He (don't, doesn't) want to sell the lake lot he owns.
2. (Isn't, Aren't) your family planning a party for the holidays?
3. The player of the drums (hasn't, haven't) improved very much.
4. There (wasn't, weren't) any cakes left after the bake sale.
5. (Who's, Whose) going with us on the trip Sunday?
6. I know that (its, it's) a long trip, but I think you will enjoy it.
7. (There's, Theirs) the first hurdle that all drivers must pass.
8. Yes, (you're, your) likely to see many relatives in that state.
9. There (aren't, isn't) any excuses for rudeness.

10. I wonder (whose, who's) picture will appear in the next issue of the newsletter.
11. The members of that church group (haven't, hasn't) held a meeting yet.
12. You can find the road; (it's, its) beyond that hill.
13. (It's, Its) too bad that the child lost (it's, its) balloon.
14. I heard that (they're, their) selling (they're, their) lovely home.

Practice 2

Mark out each incorrect word.

1. (Its, It's) time for us to clean (its, it's) cage.
2. (Your, You're) sure that we are to go to (your, you're) house, aren't you?
3. (Their, They're) new home certainly will add to (their, they're) enjoyment.
4. (Whose, Who's) the person you think will win the election?
5. (Your, You're) wife said that she would bring (your, you're) lunch.
6. (There's, Theirs) the house that Mandy said was (there's, theirs).
7. (Its, It's) tooth was chipped, but I think (its, it's) okay.
8. (Your, You're) method of working (your, you're) income tax makes me nervous.
9. When will you file (your, you're) complaint with the Better Business Bureau?
10. The doctor said (your, you're) to go to (your, you're) home tomorrow.

Practice 3

Underline each verb twice. There may be more than one in each sentence.

1. You will be surprised when I tell you this secret.
2. They might have been injured if they had not moved so quickly.
3. The day grew dark; thunder rolled through the air.
4. Mile after mile they struggled through the muddy swamp.
5. The kitten sat up, opened its eyes, and yawned.
6. Each of the birds that came to the tray for food was beautiful and small.
7. Although Ben had not sung his solo, we had to leave the auditorium.
8. Don't forget to write to us when you arrive in London.
9. Only one of the miners had drunk from that spring.
10. When my grandparents needed their old deed, we searched the attic carefully.
11. If I have seen a sunset more beautiful, I do not remember it.
12. If Carlos had built a better fence, his dog would not have gone into the street.
13. Mr. Tracy was an armchair traveler; he knew everything important.
14. The whistle has often blown early, but it never has blown late.
15. There are several old-fashioned, horse-drawn buggies in St. Augustine, Florida.
16. An apprenticeship period is not necessary on every job, but some trades require it.
17. The walls of the house were logs, the roof was straw, and the floors were dirt.
18. Did you and your friend leave early when the party became so noisy?
19. Their children certainly have grown rapidly and have become young adults.

Directions: Choose the correct words. Blacken the numbers to the right that correspond to your choices.

1. There (is, are) many people who (has, have) signed up.
   1   2   3   4

   ① ② ③ ④

2. I need to (lie, lay) down and rest before I (set, sit)
               1   2   3   4

   the table.

   ① ② ③ ④

3. Will you (teach, learn) me to swim if I will (learn, teach)
              1   2   3   4

   quickly?

   ① ② ③ ④

4. That choir on the buses (sing, sings) beautifully and
                            1   2

   (travel, travels) all over the country.
    3   4

   ① ② ③ ④

5. You (was, were) to be the candidate, but neither your
        1   2

   credentials nor your interest (was, were) sufficient.
                                  3   4

   ① ② ③ ④

6. Here (is, are) the group of trees to be planted, but many
         1   2

   (is, are) not healthy.
    3   4

   ① ② ③ ④

7. Either you or Pat (is, are) to work tonight, but there
                      1   2

   (is, are) a standby if neither of you is well.
    3   4

   ① ② ③ ④

8. (There's, Theirs) the person in the shadows who (is, are)
    1   2   3   4

   a private detective.

   ① ② ③ ④

9. He and she always (tell, tells) me when (its, it's) time
                      1   2   3   4

   to quit work.

   ① ② ③ ④

10. (Whose, Who's) the person who (has, have) welded this
     1   2   3   4

    pipe incorrectly?

   ① ② ③ ④

11. I (set, sat) on the porch and watched my wife (set, sit)
       1   2   3   4

    out the plants.

   ① ② ③ ④

12. Each of you may (chose, choose) the chair where you
                     1   2

    would like to (set, sit).
                   3   4

   ① ② ③ ④

13. What they (did, done) was wrong, but they have
               1   2

    (wrote, written) a letter of apology.
     3   4

   ① ② ③ ④

Nouns

Lesson I	**Common, Proper, and Collective Nouns**

A noun is the name of a person, place, or thing. A proper noun begins with a capital letter. The noun that names any of a class of things, not a particular thing, is called a common noun. Most nouns are common nouns.

The following review will emphasize the common and the proper noun.

Common	**Proper**	**Common**	**Proper**
man	Mr. Braddock	school	Clay Adult School
town	Topeka	group	Optimist Club
street	Bay Street	document	Magna Carta
building	White House	title	Dr. Milsap

Practice 1

Underline each noun. Write **C** over each common noun and **P** over each proper noun.

1. Santos Garza filled out an application at Low's Department Store.

2. This statement from the First National Bank is incorrect, for a large deposit made in early May was not recorded.

3. Joan showed us the brochure about the tour to France and Switzerland.

4. Wheat is grown in Kansas and a number of other states in the Middle West.

5. Dr. Vincent admitted my friend to the hospital after he had chest pains.

6. They went to Disneyland during their recent trip to California.

7. The Brown Building is located at Market Street and Main Street.

8. Tell the manager of the store that you will write your complaints to the central office in Miami.

Identifying and Using Collective Nouns

A **collective noun** refers to a group or a collection of people or things considered as one unit. A noun may be common or proper and also be a collective noun. It is important to study collective nouns because there must be subject-verb agreement in a sentence.

■ **A collective noun usually takes a singular verb. When several horses are called a *herd*, the herd is usually thought of as only one unit and will probably serve as the subject of a singular verb.**

A herd of cattle stands near the gate. The crew is at work on the bridge. A school of fish was beside the boat. The pride of lions is hunting.

■ **A collective noun requires a plural verb when each individual of a collection or group acts separately.**

The team were putting on their shirts.

Practice 2

Underline each collective noun subject once and each verb twice. Write **S** in the blank at the end of the sentence if a singular verb is used. Write a **P** if a plural verb is used.

1. Chiang's family is going to Seattle on Saturday. _____

2. The jury were angry with each other. _____

3. The new class were in their places. _____

4. The group of youngsters shouts at each newcomer. _____

5. The company is raising its requirements for applicants. _____

6. A committee from the union was meeting with them. _____

7. Wait! The choir is singing the last song. _____

8. The audience was enthusiastic and responded warmly. _____

9. Our bowling team plans to participate in the tournament. _____

10. The flock flies high over these marshes. _____

11. A group from my area takes a bus tour each year. _____

12. The army no longer marches on its stomach. _____

Plural Nouns

All nouns have number. That is, nouns may be *singular* (naming one thing) or *plural* (naming more than one thing).

■ **Many nouns form their plurals by adding -s to their singular forms.** When any singular noun ends in a sound with which -s can unite without forming a separate syllable, only -s is added to form the plural.

cab—cabs   chair—chairs   plow—plows   ink—inks

■ **Most nouns ending in sh, ch, s, x, or z are made plural by adding -es.** One exception is the word ox. Ox is made plural by adding -en to the singular word.

Singular	Plural	Singular	Plural
church	churches	flash	flashes
tax	taxes	glass	glasses
mass	masses	topaz	topazes

■ **If a vowel (a, e, i, o, or u) precedes a y at the end of a word, only -s is added to the word.**

toy—toys   key—keys   bay—bays

■ **If the y at the end of a word is preceded by a consonant (all letters except a, e, i, o, u), the y is changed to i and -es is added.**

baby—babies   sky—skies   cry—cries

■ **If the o at the end of a word is preceded by a vowel, only -s is added.**

radio—radios   cameo—cameos   portfolio—portfolios

■ **If the o at the end of a word is preceded by a consonant, the plural is formed by adding -es.**

potato—potatoes   hobo—hoboes   memo—memoes

EXCEPTION: Musical terms and instruments form their plurals by adding -s, disregarding all other rules.

■ **Almost all nouns that end in f or fe form their plurals by adding -s.** There are fourteen exceptions to this rule: *beef, calf, elf, half, leaf, self, shelf, thief, wolf, knife, life, wife, loaf,* and *sheaf.*

half—halves   knife—knives   life—lives

■ **Some nouns form their plurals by a change in the spelling of the word. Among these words are *mouse, goose, foot, child,* and *woman.***

mouse—mice   goose—geese   child—children   woman—women

- Some nouns have the same form in both the singular and the plural.

  deer   sheep   trout   moose

- Some nouns are always plural and require plural verbs.

  tongs   pants   pliers   thanks   scissors   acoustics   gymnastics

- Some nouns are plural in form but singular in meaning and usually require a singular verb.

  news   measles   mathematics   mumps   physics   civics

- **Compound words usually form their plurals by adding -s to the principal parts of the words.** *Fathers-in-law* is the plural of *father-in-law*. There are some compound words that change both parts of the compound, as in *manservant—menservants*.

Practice 1

Write the plural form of each noun.

1. half _____

2. goose _____

3. knife _____

4. sheep _____

5. boy _____

6. piano _____

7. chair _____

8. lady _____

9. tomato _____

10. pass _____

11. box _____

12. ox _____

13. man _____

14. tear _____

15. child _____

Practice 2

Write the correct plural in each blank following a singular noun.

In the deep, dark jungle _____ of the tropical country _____,

many animal _____ lived. In the thick tree _____ hundred

_____ of monkey _____ chattered away their happy life

_____. Among the animal _____ there were no kangaroo

_____ or deer _____. No hungry moose _____ ate

the bark from the limb _____. Of course, the clear water

_____ of nearby pool _____ were filled with fish

_____ of every kind. Lazy trout _____ hid themselves under

pile _____ of dead bush _____, but no fisher _____

_____ came to catch them. As the weather changed, large flock

_____ of wild goose _____ came to the land, but these noisy

bird _____ bothered the happy monkey _____ very little. How-

ever, when lion _____, tiger _____, or panther

_____ crept through the brush, all the animals would silence their voice

_____ for several second _____; and then they would scurry

for their shelter _____. The monkeys would remain in their haven

_____ of refuge and would watch the beast _____.

Practice 3

Underline each noun. Over each noun write **S** if it is singular or **P** if it is plural.

Detroit, the largest city in Michigan and known as the automobile capital of the nation, is an interesting city to visit. Besides gleaming show windows that display the latest automobiles, there are many other attractions that appeal to visitors. The Detroit Zoological Park contains wild animals that live in outdoor settings without bars or cages. In Greenfield Village—located in Dearborn, a suburb of Detroit—are many historic buildings brought to the area and restored by Henry Ford. Crafts by American artists and a fine display of old and new automobiles are exhibited nearby in the Henry Ford Museum. Detroit has many parks for recreation, including the beautiful Belle Isle, an island in the Detroit River. One popular attraction is Renaissance Center, with its four tall office buildings, a 73-story hotel, and shopping malls.

San Francisco, a fascinating port in California, is the favorite city of many Americans. Perhaps the most colorful part of the city is Chinatown, a section of San Francisco that every visitor should experience. Its narrow streets, Oriental architecture, and interesting shops and restaurants create an atmosphere not found in any other American city. A drive across the Golden Gate Bridge, a fish dinner at Fisherman's Wharf, a visit to Nob Hill, a dinner at a Chinese restaurant, and a ride on a cable car are a few of the experiences that visitors will long remember. There are also many fine parks and museums in the city. Fans of classical music might attend a concert or one of San Francisco's famous opera productions.

Lesson III Possessive Nouns

The possessive form of a noun (or a pronoun) shows possession, ownership, or connection by naming *who* or *what* possesses the second noun. There are two main rules used in forming possessives of nouns.

- **To form the possessive of any singular noun, add an apostrophe and -s.**

  mother—mother's   poet—poet's   baby—baby's

- **To form the possessive of almost all plural nouns, add an apostrophe after the final *s* that was added to make the noun plural. Not all singular nouns add -s or -es to form their plurals. Treat these nouns as singular nouns and add an apostrophe and -s to form the possessive.**

Singular Noun	Possessive	Plural Noun	Possessive
boy	boy's	boys	boys'
church	church's	churches	churches'
man	man's	men	men's
mouse	mouse's	mice	mice's
child	child's	children	children's

- **Two or more nouns may be used together in the possessive case. If these nouns denote separate ownership, each noun must show possession. If Mrs. Gay and Mr. Ander each own a large boat, then each proper noun must show possession: Mrs. Gay's and Mr. Ander's boats. If there is joint ownership, or possession, only the last noun shows possession: Jones and Brown's Hardware Store. Both people own the store.**

Separate Ownership	Joint Ownership
my uncle's and my aunt's hands	my uncle and my aunt's home
Manuel's and Ricardo's coats	Manuel and Ricardo's country

Practice 1

The sentences below contain underlined words. Circle the letter of the correctly punctuated group of words given in each group of suggested answers.

1. Only one countrys reply was acceptable to the Foreign Aid Commission.
   a. Correct as written
   b. countries' reply
   c. countrys' reply
   d. country's reply

2. The ox's yoke broke and freed both animals.

   a. Correct as written   c. oxen's yoke

   b. oxens' yoke   d. oxs' yoke

3. Three nurses' faces were all that he could see.

   a. Correct as written   c. nurses faces

   b. nurse's faces   d. nurs'es faces

4. The firefighters' helmets were as red as the blaze.

   a. Correct as written   c. firefighter'es helmets

   b. firefighters's helmets   d. firefighter's helmets

5. I cannot understand James plans for this boat.

   a. Correct as written   c. Jameses' plans

   b. James's plans   d. Jame's plans

6. Mother and Father's cars are identical.

   a. Correct as written   c. Mothers and Fathers cars

   b. Mother's and Father's cars   d. Mothers' and Father's cars

7. Antlers from several kinds of deer's heads hung in the trophy room.

   a. Correct as written   c. deers heads

   b. deers' heads   d. deers's heads

8. Leroys concept of sportsmanship gained him many friends.

   a. Correct as written   c. Leroy's concept

   b. Leroys's concept   d. Leroys' concept

9. Our guest was a well-known writer of children's books.

   a. Correct as written   c. childrens's books

   b. childrens' books   d. childrens books

The possessive case of nouns may be used in the place of a phrase that begins with *of*. Instead of saying the *works of the poet,* we say the *poet's works*. If the possessive case seems to be awkward, use a phrase in the sentence.

Practice 2

Change each phrase to the possessive case.

1. hat of man   _____   5. claws of cat   _____

2. husband of Jane   _____   6. job of employee   _____

3. garden of Lucy   _____   7. army of country   _____

4. report of officer   _____   8. books of child   _____

Lesson IV Uses of Nouns

A noun used as a predicate nominative (predicate noun) renames the subject. It follows a being or linking verb. Some of these verbs are *am, is, are, was, were, be, will be, shall be, has been,* and *have been.*

Nouns Used as Predicate Nominatives

■ **A predicate nominative may be compound, or it may be a series of nouns.**

Benjamin Franklin was a writer, a diplomat, and a scientist.

Leaves are food factories for the trees.

Practice 1

Underline each predicate noun in the following sentences.

1. The Bill of Rights is an important part of the Constitution.
2. John F. Kennedy was a president of the United States.
3. Hector will be secretary of this committee.
4. Julia was the first person on our block to run for the city council.
5. The break in his leg is a severe fracture.
6. The House of Representatives is a branch of the federal government.
7. Land to the west was once a wilderness.
8. The three largest states in land area are Alaska, Texas, and California.

Nouns Used in Direct Address

When you call a person by name, you are using a direct address.

Beth, you have completed only one test.
You are right, Chester, that I am late.
Please send this message at once, Miss Allison.

Practice 2

Underline each noun used in direct address.

1. My friends, we must close the debate and take a vote now.
2. You can count on all of us to work to the best of our abilities, Ms. Gonzales.
3. Take this box, Mary, and carry it to the loading dock.
4. Step right up, folks, and see the eleventh wonder of the world.
5. Ladies and gentlemen, it gives me great pleasure to introduce my friend, Carlos Artega.

Underline the subject nouns, nouns used in direct address, and nouns used as predicate nominatives. Write **S** over the subjects, **DA** over the nouns in direct address, and **PN** over the predicate nominatives. Do not identify the other nouns or the pronouns used as subjects.

1. Ruth, this fair is a civic responsibility, and you should do your part.

2. Charles Atlas was once a famous strongman and physical culture expert.

3. When Elizabeth became queen, India was a free nation.

4. *Cupful, handful, spoonful,* and *carload* are units of measure.

5. George, the flowers on the table came from our yard.

6. The University of Iowa is the largest higher-educational school in the state.

7. Tea has been a drink preferred by the English since 1657.

8. Boating and fishing are very popular sports on most lakes.

9. The president is the commander-in-chief of the armed forces of our country.

10. The word is a verb, but it is sometimes used as a noun or an adjective.

11. The original pedagogues were slaves who cared for their masters' young sons.

12. Mathematics is a subject that has always been difficult for me.

13. Chicago is an exciting city to visit.

14. Tornadoes are dangerous storms that can cause great damage.

15. Never stand here, Boris, for there is danger from falling objects.

16. Juan is the owner of that new car on the corner.

17. Doris is the person who called you, Don.

18. The White House is the president's home.

19. Tomas was correct, Phil, about how dangerous the trip would be.

20. After Marta became a state senator, she moved to the capital city.

21. The flavors of the ice cream were vanilla, chocolate, and peach.

22. Herb will become a fine mechanic if he continues to learn so fast.

Lesson V Nouns Used as Objects

A noun that receives the action of a verb is the object of the verb. There are two kinds of nouns as objects—indirect and direct. An indirect object will not be found in a sentence without a direct object. However, a direct object may be used without an indirect object.

Nouns Used as Objects of Verbs

■ **The noun (or pronoun) that receives the action of a verb is a direct object. Direct objects may be found by asking *who* or *what* after the verb.**

Mr. Baker answered. (Answered what?) Joan called. (Called whom?)

Mr. Baker answered my question. Joan called the doctor.

■ **In some sentences another noun (or pronoun) may come between the action verb and the direct object, showing for whom or to whom something has been done. This noun (or pronoun) is called the indirect object. An indirect object always has an understood preposition before it.**

Three television stars promised (to) Judy their assistance.
Give (to) Phil the gloves. Make (for) Donna some cookies.

Practice 1

Underline the direct objects in the following sentences. Circle the indirect objects. Some sentences have more than one direct object.

1. Her grandparents have promised Gay a car if she passes the GED test.

2. From our vacation trip we brought memories of our wonderful West.

3. The car hit the curb and swerved onto a lawn.

4. Visiting boaters can purchase a five-day permit for a small fee.

5. When John Hancock signed the Declaration of Independence, he was the president of the Congress.

6. Every year workers pay millions of dollars into retirement funds.

7. They gave their children much of the property that they owned.

8. The Yosemite's firefalls delight hundreds of people each year.

9. Did the supervisor give Stan the proper instructions?

10. I listened as the old man told Betty a story.

11. The old Spanish toast wished us health, wealth, and time to enjoy them.

12. If you take a trip today, you can rent any mode of transportation.

13. The War of 1812 greatly stimulated migration to the West.

14. The United States has shown friendliness to England and interest in its problems.

15. Fold the tent, pack the boxes, and give Mary the car keys.

Practice 2

Write sentences as directed.

1. Write a sentence that contains a direct object. Underline the direct object.

   _____

2. Write a sentence that contains two direct objects. Underline the direct objects.

   _____

3. Write a sentence that contains a direct object and an indirect object. Underline the direct object and circle the indirect object.

   _____

4. Write a sentence that contains two indirect objects. Circle the indirect objects.

   _____

Nouns Used as Objects of Prepositions

A noun (or pronoun) may also be used as the object of a preposition. It will follow a preposition and complete the prepositional phrase. Some frequently used prepositions are *as, by, at, to, for, of, with, in, down, across, through, over, during, after, on, before,* and *from.* Prepositional phrases begin with a preposition and end with a noun or a pronoun.

     OP   OP
We came (on the bus) (with our friends) last week.

     OP   OP   OP
The house (at the end) (of the street) belongs (to the town's oldest resident).

Practice 3

Put parentheses ( ) around each prepositional phrase.

1. Millions of people witnessed on television an astronaut's first step on the moon.
2. The movement of the tide brought water across the sand and over the wall.
3. The person in the wheelchair is the manager of this office.
4. He knows about the United States and about the country's way of life.

5. Down the side of the mountain came the strange caravan of nomads.
6. The appreciation of literature depends on the mood of the reader.
7. The suggestion box at the plant is used often by the employees.
8. The woman made a reputation for herself in the Air Force.
9. During the Revolutionary War, many settlers fled across the mountains.

Nouns Used as Appositives

When studying the uses of the comma, you learned that a comma (or commas) sets off an appositive from the rest of the sentence. An appositive is a word or a group of words that renames a person or thing. The appositive in a sentence could be omitted without changing the basic sentence, though the reader might lose some useful information.

Dr. Johnson, the leader of our political group, is leaving town.
The call went out for patriots, people willing to fight for justice and freedom.
Please hand this to John, the man by the window.
This is Mrs. Lopez, one of my son's teachers.
The car hit my tree, the first thing I ever planted.

A single word appositive is not usually set off by commas.

My brother Ted is an honor student at the university.

Practice 4

Underline and punctuate the appositives in the following sentences.

1. The street a broad thoroughfare really is an avenue.
2. The house a colonial mansion stands on the summit of a high hill.
3. Germany a country in Europe was once overrun by the Huns a warlike tribe.
4. The Liberty Bell the most famous bell in our country may be seen in Philadelphia.
5. If you plan to travel in Mexico our neighbor to the south you should purchase Mexican insurance.
6. Our state's *Vehicle Code* a book of highway rules is seldom read by motorists.
7. One of our magnificent sights is the Grand Canyon a masterpiece of erosion.
8. Mark Twain the author lived near the Mississippi River.
9. Few people live in Alaska a land of many contrasts.

Practice 5

Underline and identify each noun by using the following abbreviations: **S**—subject; **DA**—direct address; **PN**—predicate nominative; **DO**—direct object; **IO**—indirect object; **OP**—object of a preposition; **A**—appositive; and **P**—possessive.

1. Animals roamed over the plains of America before people crowded the land.

2. Her father-in-law is interested in her business and in her social success.

3. People living during the Dark Ages had few advantages and few comforts.

4. Ms. Smith is the secretary-treasurer of our club, but she would have made a better president.

5. Mrs. Garcia and her daughter attended the lecture, a discussion on Greek art.

6. The first money in our country was Indian wampum, beads made of sea shells.

7. Your "pieces of eight," Milton, were originally Spanish coins that were often found in colonists' pockets.

8. The fly ball was caught by the pitcher, and she threw to third base for the second out.

9. If your son is a poor reader, Carl, he may have developed incorrect eye movements.

10. The squad car brought the lifeguard a resuscitator that was to be kept near the beach.

Practice 6

Write sentences as directed.

1. Write a sentence that contains an appositive to the subject. Underline the appositive. _____

_____

2. Write a sentence that contains an appositive to the predicate nominative. Underline the appositive. _____

_____

3. Write a sentence that contains an appositive to the direct object. Underline the appositive. _____

_____

4. Write a sentence that contains a noun of direct address. Underline the noun. _____

_____

Directions: Each underlined noun is labeled as subject (**S**), possessive (**P**), predicate nominative (**PN**), direct address (**DA**), object of a preposition (**OP**), direct object (**DO**), indirect object (**IO**), or appositive (**A**). If one or more nouns are labeled incorrectly, blacken the number or numbers to the right that correspond to the error or errors. If there is no error, blacken space 5.

1. You can give **Mary** (IO, 1) the most difficult **jobs** (DO, 2) for she can work
   circles (DO, 3) around John and **Cindy** (DO, 4).   **no error** (5)   ① ② ③ ④ ⑤

2. **Agatha's** (DA, 1) main **concern** (DO, 2) was about the poor **attitudes** (OP, 3) of her
   coworkers (OP, 4).   **no error** (5)   ① ② ③ ④ ⑤

3. **Santos** (S, 1) will be the first **person** (PN, 2) in his **family** (OP, 3) to travel
   outside the **United States** (OP, 4).   **no error** (5)   ① ② ③ ④ ⑤

4. The supervisor gave **Bill** (IO, 1) and **Herb** (IO, 2) the **task** (S, 3) of cleaning
   out the bins in the storage **room** (OP, 4).   **no error** (5)   ① ② ③ ④ ⑤

5. The Indian, a **member** (A, 1) of the Navaho **tribe** (OP, 2), is the best
   speaker (IO, 3) at the **meeting** (OP, 4).   **no error** (5)   ① ② ③ ④ ⑤

6. From the **top** (OP, 1) of the **cliff** (OP, 2) came the **cry** (S, 3) of the lost
   child (OP, 4).   **no error** (5)   ① ② ③ ④ ⑤

7. **Marty** (S, 1), do you think that the **car** (S, 2) will keep running until
   Kent (S, 3) reaches **Tucson** (DO, 4)?   **no error** (5)   ① ② ③ ④ ⑤

8. Give **Rose** (IO, 1) and **Linda** (IO, 2) the **key** (DO, 3) to our **apartment** (DO, 4).
   no error (5)   ① ② ③ ④ ⑤

Pronouns

Kinds of Pronouns
Function of Pronouns

A pronoun is a word that takes the place of a noun. If there were no pronouns, we would have to use only the noun to refer to a person, place, or thing. The noun that stands for a pronoun in a sentence is called the antecedent.

■ **A pronoun must have an antecedent, a noun to which it refers. A pronoun must agree in number with its antecedent.**

Nina wanted <u>Nina's</u> mother to go with <u>Nina</u> to the movie.
Nina wanted <u>her</u> mother to go with <u>her</u> to the movie.

In the second sentence *Nina* is the word that stands for all the pronouns in the sentence. The word *antecedent* is composed of the Latin word *ante* (before) and the word *cedent* (going). Notice the circled antecedents and the underlined pronouns in the sentences below.

The (dog) hung <u>its</u> head as <u>it</u> crept away.

To reach <u>its</u> destination, the (train) must climb the mountain.

Each (man) must sign <u>their</u> time card. (Incorrect. The plural *their* cannot refer to the singular antecedent *man*.)

Practice 1

In the following sentences, underline each pronoun and circle its antecedent. If the pronoun is used incorrectly, mark it out and write the correct pronoun above it.

1. Carlos and Virginia will have to finish their work before they can leave.

2. Each woman showed their pass before entering the building.

3. Mandy, you must have your car inspected this month.

4. Each dog on that farm has had their vaccinations.

5. That hospital has its own generator in case there is a power failure.

Mark out the incorrect pronoun. Find the pronoun's antecedent before making your choice.

1. Each politician in the race will have five minutes at the beginning of the debate to state (his, their) views.
2. Everyone in those two women's clubs is going to give (her, their) contribution to the rummage sale.
3. The men in that truck have (his, their) ladders with them.
4. Each of the horses now has (its, their) feed.

Nominative Pronouns

■ **The personal pronouns *I*, *he*, *she*, *we*, and *they* may be used as subjects, predicate nominatives, appositives or with a predicate nominative.**

He is my friend. (subject)
The girl who answered was she. (predicate nominative)
Two employees, Rita and he, have worked here for ten years. (appositives to subject)

A common error is the use of an incorrect pronoun as a predicate nominative. Remember that the subject and the predicate nominative use the same type pronoun. Since the subject and predicate nominative in a sentence can exchange places with the meaning of the sentence usually remaining the same, it is easy to check to see if the correct pronoun has been used.

The last caller was she.   The winners are he and I.
She was the last caller.   He and I are the winners.

The personal pronouns *you* and *it* may be used as nominative pronouns, or they may be used as objective pronouns.

Objective Pronouns

The personal pronouns *me*, *him*, *her*, *us*, and *them* are used as (1) a direct object of the verb, (2) an indirect object of the verb, (3) an object of a preposition, or (4) an appositive to one of these objects.

Did someone call me? (direct object)
Barbara gave her the message. (indirect object)
Please send for them. (object of a preposition)
The jobs were given to my brothers, Santos and him. (appositive to object of a preposition)

Possessive Pronouns

The personal pronoun shows possession or ownership by a change in the word. An apostrophe and *s* are never added to the personal pronouns. The possessive personal pronouns are *my, mine, your, yours, his, her, hers, its, our, ours, their,* and *theirs.*

Our manager gave <u>her</u> approval of <u>our</u> plan.
The book is <u>mine</u>; the pencils are <u>hers</u>.

Practice 3

Mark out the incorrect word or words in each sentence.

1. Raymond and (I, me) are working on the same job.
2. Do you expect (us, we) to pick all those apples?
3. Dr. Temples said (me, my) method of brushing teeth is fine.
4. Does (she, her) work harder with (they, them)?
5. The fault is neither (their's, theirs) nor (our's, ours).
6. I can never trust (they, them) with important matters.
7. (We, Us) surveyors expect to work on the project all summer.
8. Was it (her, she) who caught (your, you're) fly ball?
9. Do you think they will go with (we, us)?
10. When you answer say, "This is (she, her)."
11. The last person to finish the race was (he, him).
12. You shouldn't have told that crazy story about (I, me).

Personal Pronouns Used as Compound Elements

■ **A common mistake is made with the use of two pronouns or a noun and a pronoun as a compound predicate nominative, a compound subject, a compound object, or a compound appositive.**

Study this compound predicate nominative:

The members who attended were <u>Mrs. Collins</u> and <u>I</u>.

Did you want to say *me*, not *I*? Reverse the sentence, and you will have this statement:

Mrs. Collins and I were the members who attended.

After you studied the sentence carefully, you would say:

Mrs. Collins was the member who attended.
I was the member who attended.
Mrs. Collins and I were the members who attended.
The members who attended were Mrs. Collins and I.

Study the following compound subject:

<u>She</u> and <u>I</u> are going to take the final test on Tuesday.

If in doubt about the correct personal pronouns for the subject, cover one part of the compound subject and the conjunction, change the verb to a singular verb, and write the sentence correctly with one pronoun. Then, do this with the other personal pronoun in a compound element.

She is going to take the final test on Tuesday.
I am going to take the final test on Tuesday.
She and I are going to take the final test on Tuesday.

Practice 4

Mark out the incorrect pronouns.

1. It was Fred and (I, me) who called him yesterday.
2. Don't you want to see the presents I bought for Debra and (she, her)?
3. The union members elected Dora and (he, him) in the election yesterday.
4. The first people at the scene of the accident were Greta and (he, him).
5. You must show those photographs to Ben and (I, me).
6. He and (she, her) handle all the correspondence in the office.
7. (She and I, Me and Her) usually go to exercise class together.
8. This may be (your's, yours); (him and me, he and I) found it.
9. The two speakers, Mrs. Ross and (him, he), had never met before.
10. Give the roses to the two guests of honor, Marta and (her, she).
11. The artist showed us, Steve and (me, I), many wonderful pictures.
12. I have found little kindness in either (him, he) or (her, she).
13. Look for Wesley and (me, I) on the television program.

Pronouns Used in Incomplete Clauses

Errors are often made in the use of personal pronouns when incomplete clauses, introduced by the subordinate conjunctions *as* or *than,* are used. Complete the clause orally and use the words that would be used if the clause had been completely written. Study the parenthetical completions at the end of the sentences below.

You are not quite so lazy as I (am lazy). No one has done more than they (have done).

Pronouns Used With Gerunds

■ A pronoun used to modify a gerund must be in the possessive case. A gerund is an *ing* form of a verb that is used as a noun. Some words may be one part of speech at one time and another part of speech when used in a different way: a verb may become a noun by adding *ing* to the word. In this review course, the gerund is not studied except in connection with the pronoun. Some gerunds (noun forms) are *singing, going, acting, waiting, listening,* and *accepting.* When used in a sentence with a possessive pronoun, these gerunds would be preceded by the pronoun.

No one objects to <u>her</u> going with us.
<u>My</u> acting was certainly very amateurish.
We cannot expect <u>their</u> wanting to improve their tempers.
Do you understand <u>his</u> listening to gossip?

Practice 5

Mark out the incorrect pronouns.

1. Do you understand (his, him) telling everyone about the problem?
2. We are delighted with (you, your) winning the contest.
3. We enjoyed (his, him) singing the old lullaby.
4. You still cannot walk as fast as (she, her).
5. It was (them, their) fighting that caused the meeting to end early.
6. You can always tell a joke so much better than (I, me).

Practice 6

The following sentences contain underlined expressions. Circle the letter of the group of words that best rewrites the underlined portion given in each suggested answer.

1. Ten cars waited <u>for us, Sue and I,</u> to cross the bridge.
   a. Correct as written
   b. for us, me and Sue,
   c. for us, Sue and me,
   d. for we, Sue and I,

2. I can swim better <u>than him, but him and me</u> are the champions.
   a. Correct as written
   b. than he, but him and me
   c. than he, but him and I
   d. than he, but he and I

3. The trophy was <u>ours; us inexperienced bowlers</u> had won the tournament.
   a. Correct as written
   b. ours, we inexperienced bowlers
   c. our's; us inexperienced bowlers
   d. ours; we inexperienced bowlers

4. You work as well <u>as he, but both you and he</u> need to work a little faster.
   a. Correct as written
   b. as him, but both you and he
   c. as him, but both you and him
   d. as he, but both him and you

5. Although we agreed to <u>his going, his brother and me</u> are worried.
   a. Correct as written
   b. him going, me and his brother
   c. his going, his brother and I
   d. him going, his brother and I

6. It was <u>they who sent Al and him</u> to the old house.
   a. Correct as written
   b. them who sent Al and he
   c. them who sent he and Al
   d. they who sent Al and he

7. For <u>you and I, Tommy and them</u> would do the work.
   a. Correct as written
   b. you and me, Tommy and they
   c. you and me, them and Tommy
   d. you and I, Tommy and they

Lesson 11 Relative Pronouns

A relative pronoun connects a dependent adjective clause to an independent clause. The relative pronoun will refer to an antecedent. Below are listed the relative pronouns and the things to which they refer:

<u>Who</u> and <u>whom</u> refer only to people.
<u>Whose</u> may refer to people or to animals.
<u>Which</u> refers to animals or things.
<u>That</u> may refer to people, animals, or things.

Using the Relative Pronouns *That, Which,* and *Whose*

That usually introduces a restrictive clause essential to the meaning of the sentence. Many clauses introduced by *which* will be clauses not necessary to the meaning of a sentence.

My wrench is the only one <u>that</u> is not lost.
The cottage, <u>which</u> was built of logs, is one hundred years old.

The relative pronoun *whose* is really a possessive form of the relative pronoun *who*. *Whose* will introduce a clause, but it cannot serve as the subject of a clause. *Whose* will be followed by a noun or a pronoun, which is the subject of the dependent clause. Notice the subjects and the verbs in the following dependent clauses.

She is the leader (whose group is steadily growing.)

Those (whose training was best) are more apt to survive.

Practice 1

Use parentheses ( ) to mark each dependent clause. Underline the relative pronoun that introduces each clause.

1. That must be the animal that escaped last night.
2. Please tell me whose name was drawn at the automobile show.
3. You must tell me which shirt looks better with these slacks.
4. Who told you that I would not be coming to work today?
5. The switch that is on the left is the master switch.
6. Don't tell me now that you are sorry about your actions.
7. Didn't she tell you that she would be late coming to work today?
8. Those people whose work orders are posted may leave now.

Understanding the Relative Pronouns *Who* and *Whom*

■ The relative pronoun *who* is always the subject of the dependent clause it introduces.

He is the one (who received the majority of the votes.)

Those (who are late) must stand.

I have asked for all (who will volunteer).

The relative pronoun *whom* introduces a clause that has a subject of its own. The pronoun or noun subject will follow the relative pronoun *whom. Whom* is used as an object in a dependent clause. *Whom* may be the direct object, the object of a preposition, or an appositive to one of these objects.

She is the supervisor (whom Mr. Smith sent to you.)

Almost everyone (whom you selected) is a good jury member.

This is the English person of (whom I wrote).

Compound relative pronouns are formed by adding *-ever* or *-soever* to *who* or *whom*. This addition does not change the usage of the pronoun in any way.

You will recognize (whomever we send.) I will help (whoever works.)

Study the following sentences:

Give this note to (whoever is waiting.) Speak politely to (whomever you meet.)

You have learned that the relative pronoun *whom* can be used as the object of a preposition. In studying the last two sentences above, note that *whoever* is used after the preposition *to*. In each sentence *to* introduces a noun clause. The entire clause, *whoever is waiting,* is the object of the preposition.

In the first sentence, the relative pronoun *whoever* is the subject of the verb *is waiting*. In the second sentence, *whomever* is the direct object of the verb *meet*. The entire noun clause, *whomever you meet,* is the object of the preposition *to*.

Practice 2

Use parentheses ( ) to mark each dependent clause. Write **S** over each subject and **V** over each verb or verb phrase in the dependent clauses. (Do not identify the subjects and verbs of the independent clauses.)

1. The person who won the prize will be at the awards banquet.

2. Books that tell about Africa are interesting to read.

3. Take everything that is usable back to the office.

4. Read the names of the companies whose employees will attend.

5. Many things that were given to the family were useless.

6. Helen is the only visitor whom I have not met.

7. The position that is open is not a good one.

8. Gossip that is repeated often becomes vicious.

9. I sent you one helper who will be able to do the work.

10. We did not know to whom he was speaking.

11. Anton, who is now a citizen, immigrated to this country twelve years ago.

12. Show this letter to the secretary who is sitting at the first desk.

13. The nurse spoke in a pleasant voice, which was soft and comforting.

14. The whistle, which now hangs in the mill, has not been blown for years.

15. She never forgot her old home that had been destroyed.

16. All the workers whose names were on the overtime list were pleased.

17. His speech was interrupted by people who did not accept his theory.

18. The distant mountain, which rose above the city, was snowcapped.

19. All things come to those who wait and work.

20. You may vote only for those whom you represent.

21. A song, which sounded like the voices of angels, came through the trees.

22. Bring all that is needed for the first trip.

23. Stop those who are not through.

24. I know the person who is the builder of the boats that sail this lake.

25. The person to whom we were to deliver the package has left.

26. You know that I will be gone for several weeks.

27. I will sell the camera to whoever pays my price.

28. The woman who delivers papers is always on time.

29. The painting that I purchased is much too large for the room.

30. Deliver the package to whoever opens the door.

31. The police officer whom we saw is one of my neighbors.

Lesson III Demonstrative and Interrogative Pronouns

As we study *this, that, these,* and *those,* remember that these words are not always pronouns. The words may function as adjectives when they modify nouns. The following examples will illustrate the difference in the two uses of these words.

- Demonstrative pronouns—*this, that, these, those*—point out something. *This* and *these* point out things nearby. *That* and *those* point out things farther away.

  <u>This</u> is my own factory. (demonstrative pronoun)
  <u>This</u> factory is mine. (adjective)
  <u>Those</u> cannot be left at the office. (demonstrative pronoun)
  <u>Those</u> men and women are applying for jobs. (adjective)

- An interrogative pronoun is used in asking a question. The interrogative pronouns are *who, whom, whose, which,* and *what.* Interrogative pronouns must take the place of a noun. Remember that a word becomes an adjective if it modifies a noun. *What* and *which* are the interrogative pronouns that may become adjectives.

  <u>What</u> are you doing now? (interrogative pronoun)
  <u>What</u> color did you choose? (adjective)
  <u>Which</u> is your favorite car? (interrogative pronoun)

- *Who,* when used as an interrogative pronoun, will still be a subject; it will be followed by a verb.

  <u>Who</u> <u>is</u> the happiest person that you know?
   S   V

- *Whom,* when used as an interrogative pronoun, will still be an object.

  DO
  <u>Whom</u> <u>did</u> <u>you</u> <u>want</u> for an assistant?

       OP
  To whom <u>were</u> <u>you</u> <u>speaking</u>?

Practice 1

Underline and label each demonstrative (**D**) and interrogative (**I**) pronoun in the following sentences. Be careful *not* to underline adjectives.

1. This is the most expensive restaurant in the city.

2. What is to be expected of people knowing so little about their elected officials?

3. That can make no difference in my refusal of this.

4. Who is going to campaign for these poorly paid positions?

5. For whom are you saving that seat?

6. That excuse will never be accepted by those in authority.

7. I do not care for these drawings, but I do like those.

8. These belong to which of your employees?

9. Who caught the most fish during the contest?

10. What is the lowest price you will take for all of these?

11. Whose car was that parked at the entrance?

12. Give that another coat of paint, and it will look better than this.

13. May I have those to put into this bundle?

14. Which has the better wearing qualities?

Practice 2

Write sentences as directed.

1. Write a sentence with *this* used as a demonstrative pronoun. _____

_____

2. Write a sentence with *this* used as an adjective. _____

_____

3. Write a sentence with *what* used as an interrogative pronoun. _____

_____

4. Write a sentence with *those* used as a demonstrative pronoun. _____

_____

5. Write a sentence with *those* used as an adjective. _____

_____

6. Write a sentence with *whom* used as an interrogative pronoun. _____

_____

7. Write a sentence with *which* used as an interrogative pronoun. _____

_____

Lesson IV Indefinite Pronouns

A pronoun that does not refer to a definite antecedent is called an indefinite pronoun. Misunderstanding about the singular and the plural in indefinite pronouns causes many errors.

- **Indefinite pronouns are always singular. They are used with a singular verb and are the antecedents of singular possessive pronouns.**

each	everybody	somebody	anybody	nobody
another	one	anyone	everyone	someone
no one	either	neither	nothing	

Each is to do his own work.

Someone has left her coat on the subway.

- ***Both, many, several,* and *few* are always plural. They take a plural verb and are the antecedents of plural possessive pronouns.**

- ***All, none,* and *some* may be used with either a singular or a plural verb. They may be the antecedents of either singular or plural possessive pronouns. If the objects are grouped into one mass, the singular verb is used. If the objects can be counted individually, a plural verb is used.**

Some is leaking through the crushed corner. (singular)
Some were lost among the crowd. (plural)

- **If a sentence does not show the gender (masculine or feminine) of an indefinite pronoun, use a masculine gender pronoun or pronouns for both masculine and feminine genders to refer to it.**

Everyone must take his turn. Every woman must take her turn.

Everyone must take his or her turn.

Practice 1

Mark out the incorrect words.

1. Someone in the balcony (is, are) screaming for help.
2. Many (were, was) delayed when the ferry grounded on the sandbar.
3. I am sure that neither of the men wore (his, their) raincoat.
4. If you help one of the women, I am sure that (she, they) will help you.
5. Please announce that everyone must pay (their, his or her) dues.
6. All (was, were) present when he handed in his resignation to the president.
7. In some countries no one (is, are) allowed to say what (they, she or he) thinks.

8. Although we have many members, few (are, is) present.

9. Either (is, are) satisfactory for this simple job.

10. No one except us (know, knows) about his family and background.

11. Why everybody (expects, expect) an easy life is puzzling.

12. None of the sand (is, are) to be left in the box.

13. Some of that group (has, have) welding as (her or his, their) jobs.

14. Nothing about her last letters (was, were) said when we met.

15. All (was, were) lost when the invading army entered the city.

16. Each of the puppies (have, has) a white mark on (its, their) face.

17. None of the houses in the village (was, were) very old.

18. Nobody (feel, feels) better about his success than he.

19. Some of the grass (needs, need) cutting.

20. Are you pleased that everybody (is, are) giving so much of (his or her, their) time?

21. Several (has, have) requested permission to stay longer.

Practice 2

Write sentences as directed.

1. Write a sentence with *each* used as an adjective. _____

_____

2. Write a sentence with *each* used as an indefinite pronoun. _____

_____

3. Write a sentence with *another* used as an indefinite pronoun. _____

_____

4. Write a sentence with *another* used as an adjective. _____

_____

5. Write a sentence with *either* used as an adjective. _____

_____

6. Write a sentence with *either* used as an indefinite pronoun. _____

_____

7. Write a sentence with *one* used as an indefinite pronoun. _____

_____

8. Write a sentence with *one* used as an adjective. _____

_____

Lesson V Intensive and Reflexive Pronouns

Intensive pronouns are used to emphasize a noun or a pronoun. Pronouns ending in *self* or *selves* carry the meaning of "and no one else" and give strength to a statement or question. Notice that the intensive pronoun follows the word that it intensifies.

I am the cause of this success myself.

The fact itself is not sufficient evidence.

- **The word ending -*self* is added to the singular personal pronoun and -*selves* is added to the plural personal pronoun to create intensive and reflexive pronouns. Some pronouns to which -*self* and -*selves* may be added are in the objective case; others are in the possessive case.**

myself	herself	himself	itself	yourself
thyself	oneself	yourselves	themselves	ourselves

Reflexive pronouns reflect or turn back the action of the subject. The subject and reflexive pronouns name the same person or thing. The reflexive pronoun will be the object of the active verb or of a preposition. Never use a reflexive pronoun if the person or thing has not already been named in the subject. This misuse of the -*self* pronoun is a very common error.

He hit himself with the hammer.

Mrs. Garrett is very sure of herself.

One should not expect too much from oneself.

Rules Concerning Intensive and Reflexive Pronouns

- **An intensive or a reflexive pronoun can never be a subject or a part of a compound subject.**
- **There are no such words as hisself or theirselves.**
- **Never use an intensive or a reflexive pronoun when a personal pronoun is needed.**

Practice 1

Mark out the incorrect pronouns in the following sentences.

1. With (me, myself) I must be honest.
2. Tony, Jean, and (I, me, myself) bowl often.
3. Many of the soldiers built cabins of grass for (theirselves, themselves).

4. People who work for (themselves, theirselves) are their own masters.
5. Can they build the boat (themselves, theirselves), or do they need help?
6. A person should judge (himself or herself, oneself) carefully.
7. In the end, all of you must answer for (yourself, yourselves).
8. Most people think of (themselves, theirselves) as rather good citizens.
9. The speaker invited my wife and (me, myself) to the meeting.
10. The employer and (ourselves, we) are cooperating in this matter.

Practice 2

Mark out the incorrect words.

1. My cakes are not as good as (her's, hers).
2. This discussion is between you and (me, I).
3. My neighbor (who, whom) we invited to the party did not come.
4. (We, Us) listeners liked (him, his) in spite of his praising (hisself, himself).
5. Each of the members will visit (them, those) on (their, her or his) list.
6. I will tell you (who, whom) I sent for Ann and (her, she).
7. My friends pride (themselves, theirselves) on their wonderful gardens.
8. Mr. Doyle wrote (me, I, myself) an autobiographical sketch about (him, himself).
9. The dog hid (it's, its) bone under the front steps.
10. If I were (her, she), I would write a note to Thomas and (he, him).
11. He is the manager (who, whom) liked (they, them) very much.
12. Tell (we, us) what you want, and we will get it (ourself, ourselves).
13. Several of the group (was, were) sent to stay with (us, we).
14. Neither of the chairs (is, are) large enough for you and (I, me).

Practice 3

The sentences below contain underlined expressions. Circle the letter of the correctly stated group of words given in each group of suggested answers.

1. Our guests took care of themselves until Dan and I arrived.

   a. Correct as written
   b. themselves until Dan and me

   c. theirselves until Dan and I
   d. theirselves until Dan and me

2. This is a person who you and she will like.

   a. Correct as written
   b. whom you and she

   c. who you and her
   d. whom you and her

3. The winners were he and I; the town gave us a banquet.

   a. Correct as written
   b. him and I; the town gave us

   c. him and me; the town gave us
   d. me and him; the town gave us

4. All of the judges except you and I said their's was the best.

   a. Correct as written
   b. you and me said theirs'

   c. you and I said theirs
   d. you and me said theirs

Subjective, Objective, and Possessive Pronouns

SINGULAR PRONOUNS

Subject pronouns	Possessive pronouns	Object pronouns
I	my, mine	me
you	your, yours	you
he	his	him
she	her, hers	her
it	its	it

PLURAL PRONOUNS

Subject pronouns	Possessive pronouns	Object pronouns
we	our, ours	us
you	your, yours	you
they	their, theirs	them

UNIT REVIEW

Directions: Choose the correct pronouns. Blacken the numbers to the right that correspond to your choices.

1. The first two people at the outdoor concert were (he, him)
   1   2
   and (I, me).
   3   4   ① ② ③ ④

2. Each person must be at the airport if (he, they) wants to
   1   2
   see (they, them).
   3   4   ① ② ③ ④

3. The last two visitors, Stan and (her, she), were too late to
   1   2
   go with (we, us).
   3   4   ① ② ③ ④

4. Give Roberto and (she, her) the application blanks to fill
   1   2
   out. All the people (who, whom) we selected have taken
   3   4
   the jobs.   ① ② ③ ④

5. Each woman has the right to refuse to tell (us, we)
   1   2
   (her, their) address.
   3   4   ① ② ③ ④

6. My daughter is almost as tall as (I, me), but (I, myself)
                                  1 2   3   4

    am heavier.   ① ② ③ ④

7. My wife and (I, me) will need to drive thirty miles to visit
                1 2

    (they, them).   ① ② ③ ④
     3   4

8. This purse must be (hers, her's), unless it is
                      1   2

    (yours, your's).   ① ② ③ ④
     3   4

9. (We, Us) can count on the Smiths' getting here before
     1   2

    (they, them).   ① ② ③ ④
     3   4

10. The station attendant was the one (who, whom) reported
                                1   2

    (they, them) to the police.   ① ② ③ ④
     3   4

11. That is the dog (who, that) barks at night and disturbs
                      1   2

    (me, myself).   ① ② ③ ④
     3   4

12. (Who, Whom) do you think (we, us) should call when we
     1   2   3   4

    are in Chicago?   ① ② ③ ④

13. Between you and (I, me), I think the awards should be
                      1 2

    given to (her, she).   ① ② ③ ④
      3   4

Adjectives and Adverbs

Lesson 1 Adjectives

Adjectives modify nouns and pronouns. An adjective tells what kind of person, place, or thing a noun or a pronoun is. An adjective may also point out which one or how many. Adjectives usually come before the word they are modifying.

The ship was an <u>English</u> vessel. (what kind)
<u>This</u> factory is mine. (which one)
<u>Many</u> people enjoy the <u>annual</u> dinner. (how many; which one)

Each word below may be used as a pronoun. Most can also be used as adjectives. (Remember that an adjective modifies only a noun or a pronoun.)

another	either	each	all	much	that
everyone	their	my	our	some	those
neither	these	his	any	both	your
several	many	her	few	this	

- A predicate adjective follows a being verb and describes the subject. Predicate adjectives may be compound, or they may be in a series.

    The apple blossoms are <u>white</u> and <u>fragrant</u>. (describes the subject *blossoms*)
    The plant grew <u>tall</u>. (describes the subject *plant*)

Practice

Underline the adjectives in the following sentences.

1. The elderly woman runs two successful businesses.
2. Using swift, sure strokes, he painted a small picture.
3. Twice the diving person had risen to the surface of the blue water.
4. This simple gadget is expensive but very useful.
5. The peacock's red, blue, green, and gold feathers glistened in the sunlight.
6. Many years passed before we again visited the tiny, lovely island.

Lesson II **Adverbs**

An adverb modifies a verb, an adjective, or another adverb. Many adverbs are formed by adding *-ly* to an adjective. Such adverbs as *however*, *therefore*, *hence*, or *thus* are called conjunctive adverbs. They are often used like conjunctions to join two independent clauses.

■ **The simple adverb modifies an active verb or a verb phrase by expressing manner, place, time, degree, or number.**

She moved quietly. (manner—tells how)
I waited there for an hour. (place—tells where)
You may leave soon. (time—tells when)
I called once. (number—tells how many)
He sat very still. (degree—tells how much)

■ **An interrogative adverb introduces a sentence that asks a question. The interrogative adverbs are *where*, *when*, *why*, and *how*.**

When will you return?   How is the trunk being sent?

■ **A negative adverb denies or contradicts a statement. Some negative adverbs are *no*, *not*, *never*, *only*, *scarcely*, and *hardly*. Two negative adverbs should not be used together.**

I can scarcely believe my eyes. (correct)
I haven't no more sea shells. (incorrect)
I can't hardly see the car. (incorrect)
I can hardly see the car. (correct)

■ **Adverbs used to modify adjectives or adverbs usually tell to what extent. The list of these adverbs is not long, and you should become familiar with them.**

almost	finally	only	seldom	unusually
certainly	hardly	quite	so	usually
extremely	just	rather	somewhat	very
fairly	nearly	scarcely	too	well

Practice 1

Underline the adverbs in the following sentences.

1. Her old car caused trouble constantly, but she never complained.
2. Please step forward carefully; do not move too quickly.
3. The clerk was extremely busy, but she handled the situation effectively.
4. The field yielded almost fifty bushels of corn per acre.
5. Should we leave now, or do you wish to stay later?

6. I can seldom complete my work early, for I work very slowly.
7. Angrily the shortstop threw the ball; loudly he shouted.
8. That young person is well educated and extremely polite.
9. This is surely the best bargain that we have ever found.
10. Where will we place these unusually large statues?
11. The motors started quickly, but they soon stopped.
12. Mrs. James asked me if I had been to Canada recently.
13. The operation prolonged the person's life several years.
14. The sun was shining brightly as we hurried home.
15. The new boss spoke confidently and firmly.
16. A river ran lazily through the village where Jackson lived.
17. Mr. Tyson moved quite rapidly for a person of ninety years.

Practice 2

Write sentences as directed.

1. Write a sentence with an adverb modifying a predicate adjective. Underline the adverb. _____

_____

2. Write a sentence with an adverb as the first word. _____

_____

3. Write a sentence with an adverb as the last word. _____

_____

4. Write a sentence with an adverb that separates parts of a verb phrase. Underline the adverb. _____

_____

5. Write a sentence with a negative adverb. Underline the adverb. _____

_____

6. Write a sentence with an adverb modifying another adverb. Underline the modifying adverb. _____

_____

Lesson III Comparison of Adjectives and Adverbs

The positive, comparative, and superlative degrees are the ways to describe and compare two persons or things. The positive degree describes one person or thing. The comparative degree compares two people or things. The superlative degree compares three or more people or things.

Positive	Comparative	Superlative
tiny	tinier	tiniest
late	later	latest
happy	happier	happiest
softly	more softly	most softly

- **The positive degree describes one person or thing.**

  The man was <u>clean</u> and <u>neat</u> in his <u>new</u> suit. (adjectives)
  The trainer spoke <u>kindly</u> to the little dog. (adverb)

- **The comparative degree is formed by adding -er to the positive degree of most adjectives or adverbs with one syllable or by inserting the word *more* before the positive degree of most adjectives and adverbs with more than one syllable.**

  Mary was <u>smarter</u> and <u>more determined</u> than her sister.
  Thomas works <u>more efficiently</u> than Bill works.

- **The superlative degree is used to compare three or more persons or things. The superlative degree is formed by adding -est to the positive degree of most adjectives and adverbs with one syllable or by inserting the word *most* before the positive degree of most adjectives and adverbs with more than one syllable.**

  That book has the <u>dullest</u> cover of any I have seen.
  The mayor was the <u>most indignant</u> speaker on the panel.
  I am the <u>loneliest</u> person in town. (Note that the two-syllable adverb *lonely* does not follow the rules.)

- **There are a few adjectives and adverbs that change the word when forming the comparative and superlative degrees.**

  little less least   good better best   bad worse worst

- **When a short word ends in a consonant preceded by a vowel, the last consonant is doubled before -er or -est is added.**

  sad   sadder   saddest

68

- **In words that end in -y preceded by a consonant, change y to i before -er or -est is added.**

  crazy   crazier   craziest

- **Do not make the mistake of adding an -er or an -est to the end of a word and inserting more or most before the same word.**

  Incorrect: more crazier   most craziest

- **Some adjectives and adverbs cannot be used in comparisons.**

  unique   second   the   an   two

Practice 1

Give the comparative and superlative degrees of the following adjectives and adverbs. If a word cannot be compared, leave the blanks empty.

Positive	Comparative	Superlative	Positive	Comparative	Superlative
1. many	_____	_____	2. stingy	_____	_____
3. little	_____	_____	4. rapid	_____	_____
5. red	_____	_____	6. good	_____	_____
7. sweet	_____	_____	8. bad	_____	_____
9. late	_____	_____	10. ill	_____	_____
11. honest	_____	_____	12. soon	_____	_____
13. happy	_____	_____	14. fast	_____	_____
15. useful	_____	_____	16. dusty	_____	_____
17. cruelly	_____	_____	18. early	_____	_____
19. quickly	_____	_____	20. new	_____	_____
21. kind	_____	_____	22. unique	_____	_____

Practice 2

Underline the adjectives and adverbs in the following sentences. Write **adj** over each adjective and **adv** over each adverb. This practice will help to prepare you for the unit review. The first one has been done for you.

     adj adv adj   adv   adj

1. This very fresh fruit is economically priced for this time of year.

2. Manuel went away after fully answering that very difficult question.

3. Joe drove his new car more carefully after his nearly fatal accident.

4. Yes, I will remember that unusually exciting event forever.

5. We learned much useful information from his interesting speech.

6. Many people from all parts of this country migrated to the California coast.

7. The champion boxer won in the second round; his competition was weak.

8. Those explorers were calm and brave, but they were also unusually careless.

9. An ideal home may be a simple cottage or a beautiful mansion.

10. We are constantly working to stop our many bad habits.

11. Why didn't you phone since you knew that you would be very late?

12. There was scarcely any food for the many people on the island.

13. It was much too dark to see the beautiful scenery that we were passing.

14. Our car broke down early in the day, and we waited for over five hours.

15. The rain steadily became worse, and the streets started to flood.

16. Sylvia has worked constantly learning how to work that new computer.

17. The person read the two pages carefully and then reluctantly signed them.

18. I certainly was pleased that she readily forgave my unfortunate remark.

19. She comes to see us now and then, and we are always very glad to see her.

20. Her last scheme was amazingly clever; her accomplishment was extremely valuable.

21. Maria, this bus schedule is definitely too old to be of any use.

22. The extensive damage to the car was almost completely covered by insurance.

23. We have recently remodeled our apartment at great expense.

24. Maurice repeatedly uses poor grammar in speaking, but he can usually write beautifully.

25. The most difficult job today was given to Lucy.

26. Can you accurately describe the people who attempted the robbery, or were their features too obscured by the poor lighting?

27. The Carlsbad Caverns in New Mexico attract many tourists each year.

28. The water was particularly refreshing after our long walk.

29. This extremely cold weather has damaged many fruit trees.

Directions: Following each sentence you will find five ways of writing the underlined part. Choose the answer that makes the best sentence. Then blacken the number to the right that corresponds to your choice. If there is no error, mark answer space 5.

1. Of the three people, she is the more dependable.   ① ② ③ ④ ⑤
   - (1) is much more dependable
   - (2) is the most dependable
   - (3) are the most dependable
   - (4) has always been the more dependable
   - (5) no error

2. Sharon is the brightest and most efficient person in the company.   ① ② ③ ④ ⑤
   - (1) the brighter and more efficient person
   - (2) the brighter and most efficient person
   - (3) the brightest and more efficient person
   - (4) the most bright and most efficient person
   - (5) no error

3. You are undoubtedly the most crazy and the most happy person I know.   ① ② ③ ④ ⑤
   - (1) the most craziest and the most happiest
   - (2) the craziest and the happyest
   - (3) the craziest and the happiest
   - (4) the craziest and the most happy
   - (5) no error

4. I can't scarcely read when I'm real tired.   ① ② ③ ④ ⑤
   - (1) can scarcely read when I'm real tired
   - (2) can't hardly read when I'm real tired
   - (3) can scarcely ever read when I'm real tired
   - (4) can scarcely read when I'm very tired
   - (5) no error

5. That is undoubtedly the most beautifulest and the largest garden I have ever seen.   ① ② ③ ④ ⑤
   - (1) the most beautiful and the largest
   - (2) the most beautifulest and the more larger
   - (3) the beautifulest and the largest
   - (4) the most beautiful and the most largest
   - (5) no error

Prepositions, Conjunctions, and Interjections

Lesson	**How Prepositions, Conjunctions, and Interjections Are Used**

Prepositions join a noun or pronoun object and another word in a sentence. A conjunction connects words, clauses, or phrases, and an interjection expresses strong or sudden emotion.

Prepositions

■ **A preposition is always a part of a prepositional phrase. A prepositional phrase will be composed of the preposition, the noun or pronoun object, and all modifiers of the object. A prepositional phrase may cause an error in subject-verb agreement if you are not careful. If you delete the prepositional phrase from a sentence, a simple sentence will usually remain.**

He knocked a fly ball (over the fence) (into the bleachers).
Our boat sank (below the water) and settled (on the soft bottom).

Some of the commonly used prepositions are listed below. Some of these words may also be used as other parts of speech, such as adverbs or conjunctions.

aboard	among	beside	for	on	under
about	around	between	from	over	underneath
above	at	beyond	in	past	until
across	because of	but	into	since	up
after	before	by	like	through	upon
against	behind	down	near	throughout	with
along	below	during	of	to	within
amid	beneath	except	off	toward	without

Practice 1

Underline each prepositional phrase in these sentences.

1. Birds flying toward the south darkened the sky just after dawn.
2. The jury of twelve people was given instructions by the judge.
3. We were surprised by the applause that came from the crowd of spectators.
4. Mrs. Blankenship's store is at the far end of the mall.
5. Because of the storms, we could not go to the concert.

6. In the afternoon we all worked in the hospital for several hours.
7. Beyond the hills the sun set in a blaze of color.
8. He arose at dawn and rang the bell in the tower.
9. All of us except Ralph walked along the river for several hours.

Conjunctions

- **A coordinate conjunction connects words, phrases, and clauses of equal rank. The five coordinate conjunctions are *and, but, or, for,* and *nor.***

  Dan <u>and</u> Charles will work, <u>but</u> Earl is ill.
  We bought several books, <u>and</u> I divided them among my nephews.

- **A correlative conjunction has the same function in a sentence as a coordinate conjunction, but correlative conjunctions consist of two or more conjunctions used together. The correlative conjunctions are *either-or, neither-nor, both-and, not only–but also.***

  <u>Neither</u> those who voted <u>nor</u> those who did not vote expected this result.
  <u>Not only</u> happiness <u>but also</u> success can be earned.

- **A subordinate conjunction is a conjunction used to join a dependent clause to an independent clause. Some subordinate conjunctions are listed below:**

after	before	than	until
although	if	that	when
as	lest	though	where
because	since	unless	while

- **A sentence containing a subordinate clause introduced by one of the subordinate conjunctions is a complex sentence. Remember that an introductory adverb clause is usually followed by a comma.**

Practice 2

Underline conjunctions and label them as coordinate (**coor.**), correlative (**cor.**), or subordinate (**sub.**).

1. Since you left, I have neither slept nor eaten.

2. Please tell me where Belinda and Bill will meet us.

3. Turn to the right at the next corner and go three blocks.

4. Either return the tools you borrowed or buy me some new ones.

5. We were late today because the traffic was so heavy.

6. Unless the weather clears, we will not mow the lawn and trim the hedge.

Fill in the blanks by adding a conjunction (or conjunctions) to each of the following sentences. Use a variety of conjunctions.

1. _____ the employees _____ their families were invited to the party.

2. The people ran, _____ they were not really frightened.

3. _____ the wind blows, the vane spins around _____ around.

4. _____ food _____ clothing were given.

5. A person should set aside time to work _____ to play.

6. _____ Henry _____ Joan enjoys picnics.

7. _____ she was capable and industrious, she received a promotion.

8. _____ our vacation ended, we returned to our homes _____ jobs.

9. Was he angry, _____ was he merely pretending?

10. Humility _____ sincerity were in his voice _____ manner.

11. The employees cannot work _____ the lumber arrives.

12. Bill _____ Carlos started working _____ the rest of the crew arrived.

13. _____ the rain destroyed the crop, we do not need to rent the machinery.

14. He may get the position, _____ he will find his job difficult.

15. We should study our country's history _____ we forget our early problems.

16. _____ you go with us _____ you stay here by yourself.

17. _____ the bus isn't running today, we must find another way to get to work.

Interjections

- **An interjection expresses strong or sudden emotion. The most commonly used interjections express joy, sorrow, pain, wonder, disgust, greeting, or surprise. An interjection is usually followed by an exclamation point.**

  Aha!   Help!   This dog is vicious!

Directions: The underlined and labeled words are conjunctions (**C**), prepositions (**P**), and interjections (**I**). Some underlined words are labeled incorrectly. Blacken the number or numbers to the right that correspond to any error or errors you find. If no words are incorrectly labeled, blacken space 5.

1. We stood <u>on</u>[P,1] deck <u>and</u>[C,2] watched the seagulls <u>and</u>[C,3] other birds dive <u>for</u>[C,4] food. ① ② ③ ④ ⑤

2. They walked <u>underneath</u>[P,1] the pier <u>until</u>[P,2] the tide changed, <u>and</u>[C,3] then they ran <u>along</u>[P,4] the beach kicking at the waves. ① ② ③ ④ ⑤

3. <u>Wow!</u>[I,1] The person <u>in</u>[C,2] that car <u>on</u>[P,3] the right is having trouble <u>with</u>[P,4] the car. ① ② ③ ④ ⑤

4. <u>Throughout</u>[P,1] the day, the weary travelers <u>and</u>[C,2] their ill animals trudged <u>through</u>[P,3] the desert <u>at</u>[P,4] a snail's pace. ① ② ③ ④ ⑤

5. <u>Neither</u>[C,1] Juan <u>nor</u>[P,2] Carla were <u>at</u>[C,3] the rally held <u>for</u>[P,4] the politician. ① ② ③ ④ ⑤

6. <u>Although</u>[C,1] the Yamamotos left on their trip today, they called <u>and</u>[C,2] asked <u>if</u>[C,3] I could attend their party <u>after</u>[C,4] their return. ① ② ③ ④ ⑤

7. Mrs. Garza told me that <u>not only</u>[P,1] Carlos <u>but also</u>[P,2] Anita would be <u>at</u>[P,3] the bus station at five o'clock <u>to</u>[P,4] meet us. ① ② ③ ④ ⑤

8. I take a plane <u>to</u>[P,1] Denver <u>and</u>[C,2] then change planes <u>for</u>[P,3] my flight <u>to</u>[P,4] Detroit. ① ② ③ ④ ⑤

Punctuation

Lesson 1 Punctuation Marks

Punctuation marks aid communication. Every punctuation mark serves a definite purpose and helps provide guidelines or clues for the reader. Changing one mark may change the meaning of a sentence.

These examples show how changes in punctuation can affect meaning.

"Thank you, John," Paul said.
"Thank you," John Paul said.

In the first quotation, Paul speaks to John by name. In the second quotation, only one man is named John Paul.

The wolf, having eaten Grandmother, crawled into the bed.
The wolf having eaten, Grandmother crawled into the bed.

In the first sentence, the wolf has eaten Grandmother and then crawled into bed. The second sentence (by omitting one comma and changing another) tells that the wolf has eaten and that Grandmother has crawled into bed.

Practice 1

Explain what is being said in each sentence.

1. Sarah Jane said, "Please leave." _____

_____

2. "Sarah," Jane said, "please leave." _____

_____

3. John Victor will sign your time card. _____

_____

4. John, Victor will sign your time card. _____

_____

5. The employee, having quit the contractor, found a new job. _____

_____

6. The employee having quit, the contractor found a new job. _____

_____

End Punctuation

End punctuation marks are perhaps the most important marks used. Study the following paragraphs. Notice the clarity of the second paragraph after just the end punctuation and the necessary capital letters have been inserted.

How high these hills were the old man struggled slowly upward would he ever reach the small cabin that stood out against the dying light

How high these hills were! The old man struggled slowly upward. Would he ever reach the small cabin that stood out against the dying light?

The period may be used as an inside punctuation mark, too. It is used following initials and abbreviations and as a decimal point.

Mr.   ibid.   U.S.A.   lb.   3.097 $6.45

Practice 2

Add any periods, question marks, or exclamation points needed in these sentences.

1. Didn't they move to the USA recently
2. Mr and Mrs Garza paid 99 cents for a lb of grapes
3. Watch out for that snake
4. Who can tell us some interesting sights to visit in Washington DC next week
5. This shirt is $1495, but that shirt is only $1295
6. Can't you tell me how to fix a flat
7. Run for your lives
8. Dr Barraza, didn't you tell me to take this medicine once a day
9. That job was too easy, and Mrs Goodman did not enjoy it
10. Please tell Dr and Mrs McNutt that I can sell them 20 lbs of shelled pecans
11. Mr and Mrs Rudy Gonzales own that department store
12. This US postage stamp is very old
13. When will we be able to buy a lb of grass seeds

Lesson II Using Commas

Two independent clauses may be joined by (1) a conjunction (*and*, *but*, *or*, *nor*,) preceded by a comma, (2) a semicolon alone, (3) a conjunctive adverb preceded by a semicolon and followed by a comma, or (4) a conjunction alone, if the two clauses are very simple or very short.

Using the Comma With Clauses

■ **Use a comma between an introductory adverb clause and an independent clause. A comma normally is not used before an adverb clause that follows an independent clause. One way to decide if a comma is needed in such sentences is to determine if you would normally pause before the adverb clause if it were read aloud. If a pause seems natural, a comma probably should be added.**

Since he is my best friend, I will do his part of the work.
He called when he passed through town.
I left, though I should have stayed a few minutes longer.

■ **Nonrestrictive adjective clauses that add interesting information not vital to the meaning of the sentence are set off by using a comma or commas. A clause necessary to the meaning of a sentence is not set off by commas.**

The man who is waiting at the door is my boss.
General MacArthur, who fought valiantly in the Pacific, was a famous general.

■ **A comma comes before a conjunction used to join two independent clauses.**

The Polish citizens heard the general's promise, but they were uneasy.

■ **A comma is often used after the words *however, moreover, for example*, and other conjunctive adverbs used to join two independent clauses.**

Practice 1

Each sentence contains a comma error. Make each group of words into a correct compound sentence by adding a conjunction after each comma blunder.

We will be late, we will be there before the speech starts.
We will be late, but we will be there before the speech starts.

1. Lupita went to work, I stayed at home. _____

_____

2. The doctor was in the operating room, her nurse was taking care of her office. _____

3. Take my hand, you might fall on this rough pavement. _____

4. You must answer the question truthfully, then you must sign the form. _____

Practice 2

Insert commas as needed. Underline each adjective clause not necessary to the meaning of a sentence. Some sentences have no unnecessary clauses and need no commas.

1. You may go if you wish though I think it is a mistake.
2. My cousin who is a good tennis player will arrive today.
3. If you are determined to succeed you will work hard for success.
4. I have worked all day, Elaine; nevertheless there is much to be done.
5. George should not be so unhappy for the hard times should not last long.
6. Harry must make a decision soon or it will be too late.
7. Allison who is never on time did not receive a raise this year.
8. When fall comes again the birds will fly south.
9. The old bell which once was rung on special occasions is still there.
10. Grandmother's furniture was old and worn but it was valuable to her.
11. Sandra was given a promotion; however it will not be reported in this newsletter.
12. We cannot accept his resignation as he alone knows the needed specifications.
13. Because many tourist attractions are offered our chief industry is tourism.
14. The house where Jefferson once lived is now a national shrine.
15. He blew the boat's whistle loudly but the bridge did not rise.
16. None of us know who the person is.
17. Since you left I have been very lonesome.
18. That woman who is at the third desk is a genius.

Other Uses of the Comma

- **Use a comma or commas to set off words in direct address. These are words that name the person or persons to whom the speaker is speaking. The name may be at the beginning, in the middle, or at the end of a sentence.**

  Mr. Steelman, I would like to speak to the group.
  There is only one holiday in September, Beverly.
  We sincerely regret, students, that we cannot do as you wish.

■ **Use a comma or commas to set off appositives. An appositive renames a person or thing already introduced and may give additional information.**

A horde of invaders, the Huns, pushed down into France and Prussia.
The old crow, a sentinel for the forest creatures, sat and watched.
We were surprised to see Mr. Tucker, our former boss.

■ **Use a comma or commas to set off an expression that interrupts the sentence. These expressions give no additional meaning to the sentence; they add color or emphasis.**

I will, thank my lucky stars, be able to accept the position.
His response, I must admit, was a shock to us all.

■ **Use a comma or commas to set off independent words such as** *yes, no, well,* **and** *indeed.* **Transitional words, such as** *incidentally* **and** *however,* **will also be set off by commas.**

Indeed, I will find a place for you.
The verdict, incidentally, does not change my opinion.
No, you should use pliers.
Well, she asked me for an honest opinion.

■ **Use a comma or commas to set off contrasting words or phrases. These words are negative expressions that do not need to be expressed as a complete sentence.**

Work, not words, is what we need.
The food was furnished by the club, not by the city.

Practice 3

Each sentence below contains an underlined group of words. Four suggested answers are given. Circle the letter of the one which is correctly punctuated.

1. Almost all jobs, however, demand education and training.
   a. Correct as written
   b. all jobs however, demand
   c. all jobs; however demand
   d. all jobs, however; demand

2. You people in the front row; please come to the room on the right.
   a. Correct as written
   b. front row please, come,
   c. front, row, please come
   d. front row, please come

3. Yes I am sure that most nations will be represented at the conference.
   a. Correct as written
   b. Yes, I, am sure that
   c. Yes, I am sure, that
   d. Yes, I am sure that

4. Indeed Nancy, we will be pleased to consider your application.

   a. Correct as written
   b. Indeed, Nancy, we will be
   c. Indeed, Nancy we will be
   d. Indeed: Nancy, we will be

5. The commissioners, not the people, selected the site.

   a. Correct as written
   b. commissioners not the people
   c. commissioners, not the, people
   d. commissioners not, the people

6. This blueprint on the other hand, is excellent.

   a. Correct as written
   b. blueprint, on the other hand
   c. blueprint, on the other hand,
   d. blueprint on the other hand

Using Commas in Series, Addresses, and Dates

- **Use a comma to separate a series of clauses, phrases, or words.**

  I called, I screamed, and I cried; but no one came to rescue me.
  I will speak to the workers, about the workers, and for the workers.
  Tall buildings, busy streets, and hurrying crowds frightened Daniel.

- **Use commas to separate names of streets from names of towns, names of towns from names of states, and names of states and their ZIP Codes from names of countries. If the name of a city is followed by the name of a state or a country, both names should be set off with commas.**

  A package from Germany was sent to 26 Bay Street, Dayton, Ohio 45430, U.S.A.

- **Use commas to separate names of days from names of months and to separate names of months and numeric dates from years. (The name of the month and the number of the day are considered one unit.)**

  Geoffrey was born on February 29, 1966, at 6:30 P.M.
  We will finish the building on Friday, July 26.

Practice 4

Insert commas as needed in the following sentences.

1. My brother's wife was born in London England twenty-nine years ago.
2. I filled out a sample form checked the figures and then copied it on the final form.
3. Dogs cats and chickens wandered aimlessly down the street.
4. That package must be declined by no later than Monday May 3.
5. My aunt lives at 1821 Druid Drive Memphis Tennessee.
6. The truck ran off the road jumped a ditch and hit a tree.
7. On March 9 1789 the Constitution became the law of the United States.
8. Bells rang whistles blew and people cried with joy and happiness.
9. From the burning forest fled deer rabbits bears snakes and other creatures.
10. The sun was low red and glowing when we reached the hilltop.

Lesson III Using Semicolons, Colons, Dashes, and Apostrophes

Semicolons, colons, dashes, and apostrophes are punctuation marks that are used for very specific purposes. These marks can help make the meaning of a sentence more clear without the use of additional words.

Using Semicolons

- **Use a semicolon to separate independent clauses when the clauses are not joined by a conjunction. These clauses usually are short and closely related.**

  The moon-worshipers raised their heads; no sound reached them.

- **Use a semicolon to separate independent clauses when such conjunctive adverbs as *otherwise, however, nevertheless,* and *consequently* are used.**

  The crew worked diligently; consequently, the dam was finished on time.

- **Use a semicolon to separate independent clauses when there is a comma within the clause.**

  The men, the women, and the children came; and many received help.

Practice 1

Insert semicolons as needed in these sentences.

1. We left home early nevertheless, we missed our bus.
2. Tom, Carlos, and Tina are on the day shift and we are on the night shift.
3. Arrive before six o'clock otherwise, you might find that all of us have left.
4. Stand still don't appear so nervous.
5. We were nervous on the other hand, we were confident.

Using Colons

- **Use a colon when a list or a series is introduced.**

  The school offered the following courses: business English, accounting, and drafting.

- **Use a colon before a formal quotation.**

  Confidently President Roosevelt stated: "We have nothing to fear but fear itself."

- **Use a colon before a clause that restates or emphasizes.**

  Her word was law: she allowed no interference.

- **Use a colon after the salutation of a business letter.**

  Dear Mr. Green: Gentlemen: Dear Sir or Madam:

Using Dashes

- **Use a dash to indicate a sudden change or break in thought.**

  She has earned my praise—but what do you think?

- **Use a dash to introduce a summary after a series of words.**

  Honor, love, respect, and praise—all of these Marshall wanted.

- **Use a dash to separate appositives and interrupting expressions from the rest of the sentence if the appositive or expression contains commas within it.**

  Will you give me the answer—needless to say, the right answer—to this problem?
  The three people—Manuel, Kathy, and George—are leaders at the plant.

Practice 2

Add colons and dashes as needed in the following items.

1. The bus goes down these streets Elm, Pine, and Maple.
2. The candidates Smith, Garza, and Washington will have a debate tonight.
3. Who made this statement "Give me liberty or give me death!"?
4. The pioneers please pay attention, folks suffered many hardships.
5. Tools, oil, water, and gloves these are the things that must be packed.

Using Apostrophes

- **Use an apostrophe to show the possessive case of nouns. (This usage is discussed in Unit 3.) An apostrophe is also used to indicate the omission of a letter or letters in a word. These words are called contractions.**

  I'm sure that he's the one who thinks that he can't fail.

Practice 3

Add apostrophes to words as needed in these sentences.

1. Im afraid youve failed to pay the insurance premium on time.
2. Dont you like the new color theyve chosen to paint their house?
3. Sandra doesnt know if shes to work today.
4. Havent you told them that this isnt a job theyll like?

Practice 4

Insert correct marks of punctuation as needed in the sentences.

1. Theyve weighed the evidence on both sides it seems to balance.
2. Home, family, security, and health these people seek.
3. If were late, please say that were coming.

4. There arent any veterans of the Civil War now living.

5. This plan and its really my own will revolutionize industry.

6. You must be responsible for these items blankets, pillows, sheets, and towels.

Lesson IV Using Quotation Marks

A direct quotation repeats the exact words of a speaker. Quotation marks enclose the words of the speaker, not the name of the speaker and the description of speaking manner. Sample sentences below show how capital letters, quotation marks, and other punctuation marks are used with direct quotations.

Punctuating Direct Quotations

"When writing a short story, you must present a basic theme," she said.
"Help! Help the child!" the mother screamed at us.
Sadly Rip asked, "Where is my wife? Where are my children?"

In a broken quotation, the name of the speaker and the description of the speaker's manner of speaking is in the middle of the quotation. If the broken quotation is within a sentence, the first word in the continuation of the quotation is not capitalized. However, it is necessary to have two complete sets of quotation marks to enclose both parts of a broken quotation. Commas separate the speaker from each side of the quotation. If the continuation of a quotation begins a new sentence, the first word is capitalized.

"Your highness," the peasant pleaded, "please spare my children."
"Those who advocate the acceptance of *ain't* are not acquainted with its history," the speaker said. "It is a corruption of an old contraction for *am not*, written *a'n't*.

Practice 1

Punctuate the following quotations, inserting quotation marks, commas, question marks, exclamation points, and periods. Insert capital letters as needed.

1. Roberto asked isn't it time to start counting the ballots

2. The boy replied no madam we do not live here now

3. Get out of my boat Bill shouted as he ran toward the water

4. Maria spoke quietly and said I saw the car when it passed

5. The water is deep said Jerry and very cold

6. Henry called to his father the car is washed and ready

7. Yea team Rah Rah shouted the crowd

8. You need to read your job description more carefully said Morris

84

9. Long ago people ate with their fingers she said there were no forks

10. No I am not going he said I do not have a car

11. The librarian said to the boys be quiet, please

12. John and I thought that he said, "I will be there."

13. Bring the water quickly the man shouted

The Indirect Quotation

An indirect quotation states what a speaker says but not exactly as the speaker said it. The indirect quotation is not enclosed in quotation marks. In the examples given below, the first sentence of each group is a direct quotation; the second is an indirect quotation.

Clarence asked, "Are you going fishing with me today?"
Clarence asked if I were going fishing with him today.
"I do not know your cousin," said Alex.
Alex said that he does not know my cousin.

Practice 2

Change these sentences that contain indirect quotations into sentences that have direct quotations.

Nick said he wants to tell us about the new job requirements.
Nick said, "I want to tell you about the new job requirements."

1. The mayor said that this project is essential to the future growth of the city. _____

   _____

2. Jane told me that she plans to resign at the end of this month. _____

   _____

3. I told you that we must finish this job before dark. _____

   _____

4. The doctor said that you need this prescription. _____

   _____

5. The pharmacist said that you shouldn't drive while taking this medicine. _____

   _____

6. The police officer said that I was driving too fast. _____

_____

7. You told me that Don is to arrive at the airport this afternoon. _____

_____

8. Sandy said that she will help me paint my bedroom. _____

_____

9. I told you that I will be unable to work on your car this week. _____

_____

10. The personnel manager said that I will need to fill out an application blank. _____

_____

11. Pat said that a bridge was washed out on Highway 12. _____

_____

12. I screamed that a snake was under the car. _____

_____

Other Uses of Quotation Marks

- **Quotation marks set off titles of stories, poems, essays, songs, and magazine articles.**

  "Old Man River" is a favorite song of mine.

- **Quotation marks are used to emphasize unusual expressions, slang words, and nicknames.**

  He used "ain't" three times in his speech.

Practice 3

Insert quotation marks where needed in the following.

1. Did you say that The Raven is your favorite poem?
2. How To Find a Job was the article in the magazine I enjoyed most.
3. Teddy is the nickname my parents gave me.
4. The Star-Spangled Banner was written in the early 1800s.
5. My real name is James, but everyone calls me Jimmy.
6. The Night the Bed Fell is a very funny story.

Directions: Study each underlined area to see if the punctuation is correct or if punctuation is needed. If there is an error or errors, blacken the number or numbers to the right that correspond to the number of the underlined part. If there is no error, blacken space 5.

1. Although we left a little late, we did arrive before the
   $\overline{1}$

   band played the Star-Spangled Banner. "   no error   ① ② ③ ④ ⑤
   $\overline{2}$ $\overline{3}$ $\overline{4}$ $\overline{5}$

2. Tony has been nicknamed "The Bee" because, he delivers
   $\overline{1}$ $\overline{2}$ $\overline{3}$

   packages all over town to businesses?   no error   ① ② ③ ④ ⑤
   $\overline{4}$ $\overline{5}$

3. Nora, don't you think that you should read the article,
   $\overline{1}$ $\overline{2}$ $\overline{3}$

   "How to Apply for a Job," before you go for your

   interview.   no error   ① ② ③ ④ ⑤
   $\overline{4}$ $\overline{5}$

4. Did you say that this package, of candy, is $1.35?
                    $\overline{1}$ $\overline{2}$ $\overline{3}$ $\overline{4}$

   no error   ① ② ③ ④ ⑤
   $\overline{5}$

5. Your daughter, who really appears to be brilliant, must be
   $\overline{1}$ $\overline{2}$

   an outstanding student, Betty.   no error   ① ② ③ ④ ⑤
   $\overline{3}$ $\overline{4}$ $\overline{5}$

6. You can sign up for the CPR course today, however, you'll
   $\overline{1}$ $\overline{2}$ $\overline{3}$

   not begin the training until the end of the month.
   $\overline{4}$
   no error   ① ② ③ ④ ⑤
   $\overline{5}$

7. This lb. of grapes costs too much money but the cost per
   $\overline{1}$ $\overline{2}$

   lb. of those cherries is ridiculous.   no error   ① ② ③ ④ ⑤
   $\overline{3}$ $\overline{4}$ $\overline{5}$

8. Mr. and Mrs. Delano were eager to see the new house, but
   $\overline{1}$ $\overline{2}$ $\overline{3}$

   they were very disappointed in the interior colors!
   $\overline{4}$
   no error   ① ② ③ ④ ⑤
   $\overline{5}$

9. "We watched the comedy, on television; they watched a
   $\overline{1}$ $\overline{2}$ $\overline{3}$

   mystery.   no error   ① ② ③ ④ ⑤
   $\overline{4}$ $\overline{5}$

Capitalization

| Lesson | **Using Capitalization** |

Capital letters are used to point out some special person, place, or thing. These capitalized words are called proper nouns or proper adjectives. The following examples illustrate some of the most important rules for the use of the capital letter.

Capital Letters With Proper Nouns and Proper Adjectives

- Always capitalize the first letter of a proper name, a day of the week, a month, or other measure of a period of time.

  Mr. Frank Waters reached Mexico on Tuesday, August 3, at 7:30 P.M.

- Always capitalize the first letter in the name of a religious sect, a state of the union, and a college or university.

  The Puritans of Connecticut originated the idea of Yale College.

- Always capitalize the first letter in the name of an important document, a historic event, or a title of a government official.

  The Constitution was not approved until after the Revolutionary War.

- Always capitalize the name of a business, a street, a product brand, or a noun standing for a name.

  The Wilderness Company on Vine Street ordered Rockpoint shoes for Father.

- Capitalize the name of a geographic region, the name for a race of people, a political party, or a special building.

  A delegation of Native Americans, representing the Southwest, met with members of the Democratic Party in the Federal building.

- Capitalize the title of a book or the title of a work of art.

  The Magic Mountain is one of Thomas Mann's best-known novels.

Mark out the letters that should be capitalized. Place a capital over each.

1. The ideas found in the iroquois confederacy of indian tribes were used in the united states constitution.

2. athens and sparta were city-states in ancient greece.

3. When a famine came to ireland during the 1800s, many irish people sailed to America.

4. We plan to read *cannery row* by john steinbeck.

5. Did you attend everest adult high school in daytona, florida, last year?

6. There were jewish, catholic, baptist, and buddhist leaders in the audience.

7. The catholic missions in south america and the american southwest were built in the same style.

8. The end of world war I did not bring lasting peace between germany and france.

9. A park, the international peace gardens, has been constructed on the border between the united states and canada.

10. On july 4, 1776, the declaration of independence was read to the american people for the first time.

11. The letter from the school was sent to 6 maple road, reno, nevada 88953; but james was not there.

12. My brother asked mother and father to take him to work this morning.

13. The torah is one of the sacred books of the world.

14. From new york, the group sailed to france on the *United States*.

15. prime minister churchill was a visitor in washington many times.

16. The meeting of democratic state governors was held in Chicago.

17. We found april and may delightful months in southern california.

Other Uses of Capital Letters

Although most capitalized words are proper nouns, some capitalization rules deal with words that are not always nouns.

■ **The first word of a sentence begins with a capital letter.**

The office doors were opened at nine o'clock each morning.

- **The first word of a line of poetry is usually capitalized.**

  Water, water, everywhere
  Nor any drop to drink.
  —*Samuel Taylor Coleridge*

- **Capitalize the interjection O.**

  Dainty fairy lace-work, O so finely spun,
  Lying on the grasses and shining in the sun.
  —*Christina Rossetti*

- **Capitalize the pronoun I.**

  Gabriel and I have studied anthropology for years.

- **Capitalize adjectives derived from proper nouns.**

  The Scandinavian countries have long, cold winters.

- **Capitalize the first word and all nouns in the salutation of a letter.**

  Please begin this letter with "My dear Sir."
  No, I believe it should begin with "Dear Madam."

- **Capitalize only the first word of a closing phrase in a letter.**

  May I use "Sincerely yours" as a closing phrase?
  You may, but you might prefer to use "Cordially yours."

Practice 2

Each sentence below contains an underlined group of words. Four suggested answers are given. Circle the letter of the one that has correct capitalization.

1. You are reading *English Essentials,* a book by Jewel Varnado.

   a. Correct as written
   b. *English Essentials,* a book by jewel Varnado
   c. *English Essentials,* a book by Jewel varnado
   d. *english essentials,* a book by Jewel Varnado

2. When Grandfather retired, he received Social Security payments.

   a. Correct as written
   b. Grandfather retired, he received Social Security Payments
   c. grandfather retired, he received social security payments
   d. grandfather retired, he received Social security payments

3. From their letter he read: "On April 18th, we traveled north into ohio."

   a. Correct as written
   b. We traveled North into ohio
   c. we traveled north into Ohio
   d. we traveled North into Ohio

90

4. Perhaps George Washington's Birthday was not on February 22.

    a. Correct as written
    b. George Washington's birthday was not on February 22
    c. George Washington's Birthday was not on february 22
    d. George Washington's birthday was not on february 22

5. "Are you hurt, Tim?" Mrs. Taylor, the supervisor of the Plant, asked.

    a. Correct as written
    b. Tim?" mrs. Taylor, the supervisor of the Plant
    c. Tim?" Mrs. Taylor, the Supervisor of the plant
    d. Tim?" Mrs. Taylor, the supervisor of the plant

6. This coffee comes from Sao Paulo, a state in the Southern part of Brazil.

    a. Correct as written
    b. Sao Paulo, a State in the Southern part of Brazil
    c. Sao Paulo, a state in the southern part of Brazil
    d. Sao Paulo, a State in the southern part of brazil

7. our guests from detroit, Michigan, will be here tomorrow morning.

    a. Correct as written
    b. Our guests from Detroit, Michigan
    c. Our Guests from detroit, Michigan
    d. Our guests from detroit, michigan

8. Oh, to be in England,/now that April's there.
   — *Robert Browning*

    a. Correct as written
    b. Now that april's there
    c. Now that April's there
    d. now that april's there

9. On Monday, September 3, our labor day parade will start from Lomax Street.

    a. Correct as written
    b. monday, September 3, our Labor Day Parade
    c. Monday, September 3, our Labor Day Parade
    d. Monday, September 3, our Labor Day parade

10. My father and I might go to New Orleans during Mardi Gras.

    a. Correct as written
    b. Father and I might go to New Orleans during mardi gras
    c. father and I might go to New orleans during Mardi Gras
    d. Father and I might go to New Orleans during Mardi Gras

11. The European Countries have many tourists in the Spring.

    a. Correct as written
    b. european countries have many tourists in the Spring
    c. European countries have many tourists in the Spring
    d. European countries have many tourists in the spring

Directions: Some underlined words may be capitalized when they should not be; other words need to begin with capital letters to be correct. Blacken the number or numbers to the right that correspond to any error or errors you find. If no words are incorrectly written, blacken space 5.

1. The shakers, members of a religious sect, are known for
   1   2

   the beautiful furniture they made.   ① ② ③ ④ ⑤
       3   4

2. Did you say that the democrats will hold a meeting of
                        1

   state governors in San Francisco, California?   ① ② ③ ④ ⑤
         2   3   4

3. Haven't mr. and mrs. Alvarez moved to the
           1   2   3

   midwest recently?   ① ② ③ ④ ⑤
   4

4. Those two french tourists said they had traveled in
               1

   California, illinois, and new york.   ① ② ③ ④ ⑤
   2   3   4

5. You can always find shoes at a reasonable price at
   Herren's Department store on Spring street.   ① ② ③ ④ ⑤
   1   2   3   4

6. Why don't you come to St. Louis and stay with us at the
                         1

   Wildflower hotel, father?   ① ② ③ ④ ⑤
   2   3   4

7. Her grandfather was a captain during world war II.   ① ② ③ ④ ⑤
       1   2   3   4

8. They were in Canada last August for several days before
                1   2

   leaving on a trip to London and Paris.   ① ② ③ ④ ⑤
                       3   4

9. The <u>Declaration</u> of <u>Independence</u> was signed long before
           1   2

   the <u>constitution</u> was written in <u>Philadelphia</u>.
        3   4   ① ② ③ ④ ⑤

10. <u>For</u> some reason, she always begins her letters with "<u>My</u>
     1   2

    <u>Dear</u> <u>Sir</u>."
     3   4   ① ② ③ ④ ⑤

11. Mr. <u>clark</u> said the new <u>author</u> was as good a writer as
         1   2

    <u>william</u> <u>Faulkner</u>.
      3   4   ① ② ③ ④ ⑤

12. Seattle, <u>washington</u>, was named for <u>Chief</u> Seattle, the
              1   2

    great <u>native</u> <u>american</u> orator.
          3   4   ① ② ③ ④ ⑤

13. <u>Horace</u> <u>greeley</u> was quoted as saying, "<u>go</u> <u>west</u>,
     1   2   3   4

    young man."
                                        ① ② ③ ④ ⑤

14. The <u>doctor</u> said <u>i</u> should be careful not to overeat during
        1   2

    the weeks between <u>thanksgiving</u> and <u>Christmas</u>.
                      3   4   ① ② ③ ④ ⑤

15. My <u>Cousin</u> and <u>I</u> took a trip by <u>highway</u> from Arizona
        1   2   3

    to <u>maine</u>.
       4   ① ② ③ ④ ⑤

Introduction to Correct Usage

Lesson 1 USAGE

The customary use of words or groups of words is called usage. Good usage is the use of acceptable language according to the rules of standard English, especially as it is written. Correct usage is a key to effective communication.

Good usage requires the following:
1. Right use of a word
2. Correct grammar
3. Clear language form
4. Effective form of expression
5. Acceptable style

Study the following words and expressions commonly misused.

■ <u>a — an</u>

A is used before words beginning with a consonant sound. (He was a very tall man.)

An is used before words beginning with a vowel sound. (Brenda is an actress.)

■ <u>accept — except</u>

Accept means to receive. (We do accept your apology.)

Except means to leave out or other than. (The story is good, if you except some errors.) (Everyone here except Patricia is a physical therapist.)

■ <u>affect — effect</u>

Affect means to influence or to change. (The wind may affect the crops.)

Effect means to bring to pass. (This method will effect great reforms.)

■ <u>aggravate — irritate</u>

Aggravate means to make worse. (We aggravated the situation by our remarks.)

Irritate means to excite or to upset. (Rudeness will irritate anyone.)

■ <u>ain't</u>

Ain't is not an acceptable contraction for any word in the English language.

- **all ready — already**

  All ready means that all are prepared. (We are all ready for the race.)

  Already means previously. (He had already completed the job by then.)

- **all right — alright**

  All right means entirely correct. (The problems are all right.)

  Alright means the same as *all right* but is not as commonly used.

- **all together — altogether**

  All together means in a group. (We are all together at last.)

  Altogether means wholly or thoroughly. (You were altogether right.)

- **almost — most**

  Almost is an adverb meaning nearly. (Almost all employees are eligible for a bonus.)

  Most is an adjective modifying a noun. (Most doctors do not make house calls.)

- **among — between**

  Among refers to three or more persons or things. (Cows roamed among the trees.)

  Between refers to only two persons or things. (Choose between good and evil.)

Practice 1

Underline the correct word or words in each sentence.

1. Her condition was (aggravated, irritated) by her unwillingness to eat a balanced diet.
2. It will be (alright, all right) to bring your husband or wife to the picnic.
3. The tornado had a devastating (affect, effect) on the small town.
4. Divide the fresh vegetables (between, among) our two neighbors.
5. That is certainly (a, an) unusual way to divide the prizes (between, among) all the contestants.
6. You have (all ready, already) told us that same story several times.
7. We will be (altogether, all together) at the reunion for the first time in ten years.
8. Stand (between, among) Stan and Pat so that I can get all of you in the photo.
9. This (ain't, isn't) the greatest car I have ever owned.
10. Yes, I am glad to (accept, except) your apology.
11. I certainly did see (a, an) animal run from the yard.
12. We are (all ready, already) to leave whenever you are.
13. It is (all right, alright) with me if you want to use my truck.
14. Do you think that they were (all together, altogether) honest with us?
15. Please do not walk (between, among) two cars.
16. (Accept, Except) my apologies for answering your question so sharply.

Match each word on the left with a definition on the right. Write the letter of the correct answer on the line next to the word.

_____ 1. accept   a. to influence or to change

_____ 2. irritate   b. to excite or to upset

_____ 3. an   c. to leave out or other than

_____ 4. all together   d. to receive

_____ 5. except   e. an adverb meaning nearly

_____ 6. effect   f. to make worse

_____ 7. almost   g. refers to three or more persons or things

_____ 8. already   h. entirely correct

_____ 9. among   i. an adjective modifying a noun

_____ 10. all ready   j. refers to only two persons or things

_____ 11. most   k. previously

_____ 12. between   l. wholly or thoroughly

_____ 13. affect   m. used before words beginning with a vowel sound

_____ 14. all right   n. in a group

_____ 15. altogether   o. used before words with a consonant sound

_____ 16. aggravate   p. to bring to pass

_____ 17. a   q. all are prepared

_____ 18. ain't   r. an unacceptable contraction for any English language word

Study the following words and expressions commonly misused.

- **anyplace — everywhere — no place — somewhere**

  Use the word *where* instead of *place*. (Children are everywhere in the park.)

- **anywheres**

  Anywheres is not a word. Drop the *-s* to form the acceptable word *anywhere*.

- **as — as if — like**

  As and *as if* are subordinate conjunctions that introduce dependent clauses. (He spoke as if he knew the country well.)

  Like is a preposition. (Those puppies all look like small bears.)

- **as — so**

  As should be used in making a positive comparison. (This is as good as yours.)

  So should be used in making a negative comparison. (My son is not so tall.)

- **at — to**

  At should be used to imply presence in. (I stayed at home Monday.)

  To should be used with motion verbs. (I went to the store yesterday.)

- **awfully**

  Awfully is misused colloquially for the adverbs *very* and *exceedingly*.

- **bad — badly**

  Bad is always used to describe a noun or pronoun. (I feel bad.)

  Badly is always used as an adverb. (He cooks the food badly.)

- **beside — besides**

  Beside means next to or close to. (She stood beside the statue.)

  Besides means in addition to. (We expected none besides the members.)

- **bring — take**

  Bring is used to indicate motion toward the speaker. (Bring the order to me.)

  Take is used to indicate motion away from the speaker. (Take this inventory to the office.)

- **bunch**

  Bunch refers to things, not people. (George brought each a bunch of grapes.)

Underline the correct word or words in each sentence.

1. You always seem to feel (bad, badly) on Monday.

2. You should learn to manage your money (like, as) we do so that you will not always be broke just before payday.

3. If those children cannot behave, they can just stay (at, to) home the next time we go (at, to) the zoo.

4. A (bunch, group) of tourists said they couldn't find (anywhere, anywheres) to stay tonight.

5. (Take, Bring) that box of garden tools to me.

6. Don't you think the swimmer is becoming (awfully, very) tired?

7. I stood (besides, beside) the road for an hour, and I was getting very (irritated, aggravated) for having to wait so long.

8. We looked (everyplace, everywhere) for the wrench that was lost sometime last week.

9. He is standing in the doorway and acting (as if, like) he owned the place.

10. This steak tastes just (like, as) it should.

11. You can laugh, but I know I left my gloves (somewhere, someplace) in this room last night.

12. The terrible destruction is (anywhere, anywheres) you look.

13. That antique dealer told me confidentially that the vase my aunt gave me is (awfully, exceedingly) rare.

14. Please stand here (beside, besides) me.

15. Believe me, you are not (so, as) heavy.

16. Believe me, you are not (so, as) heavy as I once was.

17. (Bring, Take) this box of spare parts to the room at the end of the hall.

18. He really looks (like, as if) he has seen a ghost.

19. Maria said that she certainly feels (bad, badly) today.

20. Soon we will be able to see a large (group, bunch) of tired people running down this street.

21. You wouldn't perform so (bad, badly) if you would practice more.

22. That (bunch, group) of people has been waiting for an hour for the parade to start.

23. This chocolate tastes good (like, as) a candy bar should.

24. Doesn't this roast look (like, as if) it is done?

Study the following words and expressions commonly misused.

- **burst**

  Burst is used in both present and past tenses. (He burst all of the balloons.)

  Bursted is not a word.

- **calculate**

  Calculate means to compute, not to think. (You should calculate the cost of driving your car to work each day.)

- **can — may**

  Can expresses ability. (I can do this hard job.)

  May expresses permission. (You may have three of the roses.)

- **complected**

  Complected is not a word. Use *complexioned*. (The child who won the contest is dark complexioned.)

- **could of — could have**

  Could of is not acceptable. Use *could have*. (I could have sent the magazine to you.)

- **cute**

  Cute is colloquial and is overused. Use a more effective word. (She wore an attractive dress.)

- **different from — different than**

  Different from is acceptable; *different than* is not acceptable. (The invitation that I have is different from yours.)

- **enthused**

  Enthused is not a word. Use *enthusiastic*. (Sue is enthusiastic about golf.)

- **etc.**

  Etc. means "*and other things.*" Never use *and etc.* (Bring your paper, pen, etc.)

■ **expect — suppose**

Expect means to look forward to. (I expect that there will be an unusually large crowd at the picnic.)

Suppose means inclined to believe. (I suppose that he is able to work.)

Practice

Underline the correct word or words in each sentence.

1. You certainly could (of, have) fooled me with that disguise.
2. If you would (calculate, think) how much it costs, I will see if I (can, may) afford it.
3. I (can, may) say that this job is different (from, than) the last one.
4. She is (enthusiastic, enthused) about the trip we plan to take.
5. That bubble (burst, bursted) before it was fully blown up.
6. I (calculate, think) we should stop, rest for a few minutes, get a drink of water, (and etc., etc.,) every twenty minutes.
7. Thor's skin is light (complexioned, complected).
8. (May, Can) we use your truck to move this sofa?
9. The detective (bursted, burst) into the room and arrested a suspect.
10. I (calculate, think) that I should be president by the time I am fifty.
11. People who are fair (complexioned, complected) need to be very careful about staying in the sun too long.
12. You certainly could (have, of) been more diplomatic in the answer you gave.
13. That is a (cute, charming) vase on the table.
14. Isn't this address different (from, than) the one you gave me last week?
15. I (expect, suppose) you were surprised by that statement.
16. All of us are (enthused, enthusiastic) about a vacation in the mountains.
17. I could (of, have) told you that you were making a bad decision.
18. Dogs, cats, chickens, (and etc., etc.,) ran from the yard.
19. What should we do with the light bulb that (bursted, burst)?
20. She (can, may) sing better than anyone else in our club.
21. Don't you (expect, suppose) that we should leave before noon?
22. That flood could (have, of) caused much more damage if the volunteers had not been so effective.
23. I wore a style of shoes different (than, from) the type I usually wear.
24. How could you (of, have) forgotten something so important?
25. My gloves are slightly different (from, than) yours.
26. (Can, May) I ride to work with you today?
27. Yes, I certainly (can, may) be there by eight o'clock.
28. This repair certainly could (have, of) been done more economically.

Lesson IV

Study the following words and expressions commonly misused.

- **farther — further**

  Farther concerns spatial distance. (He moved farther and farther away from the edge of the cliff.)

  Further concerns distance in time or degree. (I have no further comments to make at this time.)

- **fewer — less**

  Fewer indicates a smaller number. (I have fewer serious health problems than she.)

  Less refers to a decrease in amount. (There is less noise here.)

- **from — off**

  From indicates that something has been obtained. (Did the manager accept the list of suggestions from you?)

  Off indicates that something has been taken away. (Take the pan off the burner.)

- **funny — strange**

  Funny means humorous. (I heard a funny story this morning.)

  Strange means unusual. (A strange dog came to our kennel.)

- **good — well**

  Good is always used as an adjective. (This is a good story.)

  Well is used as an adverb except when speaking of health or appearance; it then is used as an adjective. (This is well done.) (He looks well today.)

- **in — into**

  In refers to a location within something. (The car is in the garage.)

  Into indicates motion toward the inside. (I came into the room.)

- **in back of — behind**

  In back of should never be used. Use *behind*. (Dan stood behind the curtain.)

- **its — it's**

  Its shows possession. (The group gave its approval of the site selected.)

  It's is a contraction of *it is*. (Maybe it's under the table.)

- **learn — teach**

  Learn means to receive knowledge. (I learn many things each day.)

  Teach means to impart knowledge. (Teach me the newer method of artificial respiration.)

- **leave — let**

  Leave means to go away. (We leave on the weekend.)

  Let means to allow. (Please let me borrow your notes.)

Practice

Underline the correct word or words in each sentence.

1. That certainly is a (funny, strange) way to run if you expect to run much (farther, further).
2. The dog ran (in, into) the yard from the crowded street and then stood (in, into) the driveway barking loudly.
3. (Learn, Teach) me how to clean this fish.
4. (Let, Leave) me explain how this machine works.
5. She borrowed a slide rule (from, off) Celia.
6. There are (less, fewer) people here than we anticipated.
7. We have walked (further, farther) than we planned.
8. I walked around (in, into) the garden and clumsily fell (in, into) the fish pond.
9. That dog lost (its, it's) collar in the woods.
10. I do not have to take that kind of abuse (from, off) you.
11. She looks (good, well), but because of her illness, I know she is not (good, well).
12. Juan fell from the boat (in, into) the lake.
13. Please stand (behind, in back of) me until the photo has been taken.
14. You told me that you could (learn, teach) me to speak Spanish.
15. (Its, It's) a long trip, and we must get there before (its, it's) dark.
16. Be very careful as you step (in, into) the boat.
17. She is (in, into) the room now, but she just walked (in, into) it a few minutes ago.
18. Juan found some loose change (in back of, behind) the sofa pillow.
19. It is (good, well) to see you looking so (good, well).
20. What is that (strange, funny) noise coming from the attic?
21. The (farther, further) I studied the map, the more convinced I became that we had driven (farther, further) than we should have.
22. The dog licked (its, it's) paw.
23. There will be (less, fewer) delegates at this convention.

Lesson V

Study the following words and expressions commonly misused.

- **liable — likely**

  Liable expresses obligation. (He will be liable for all injuries.)

  Likely shows probability. (It is likely that we will meet again.)

- **lose — loose**

  Lose means to misplace. (Do not lose the money that you have.)

  Loose means free or unattached. (Frank wore a loose coat.)

- **lots of**

  Lots of should be replaced by *many* or *much*. (Samuel has many friends.)

- **off of**

  Off of should not be used. Use *from* or *off*. (She leaped from the boat.)

- **party — person**

  Party refers to a group of people, never to one. (The boating party left.)

  Person refers to a single individual. (I see only one person.)

- **real — really**

  Real means true or genuine. (I have a real Australian boomerang.)

  Really is an adverb meaning very much. (She is really interested in carpentry.)

- **seldom ever**

  Seldom and *ever* should not be used together. Use *rarely*. (She rarely talks.)

- **slow — slowly**

  Slow is usually used as an adjective. (Your clock is slow.)

  Slowly is used as an adverb. (Walk slowly to the corner.)

- **sure — surely**

  Sure is always used as an adjective. (Are you sure?)

  Surely is used when an adverb is needed. (He surely is slim.)

- **try to — try and**

  Try to should be used instead of *try and*. (Please try to finish the dress.)

■ Would of — Would have

Would of should not be used. Use *would have*. (I would have given the prize.)

Practice

Underline the correct word or words in each sentence.

1. If we stay on this road, we are (liable, likely) to get lost.
2. That (person, party) is always talking about his friends.
3. This new ice cream is (real, really) quite good.
4. My aunt was injured when she stepped (off, off of) the curb.
5. Aren't there still (many, lots of) peanuts in the jar?
6. I am clumsy, but I (rarely, seldom ever) injure myself.
7. Don't tell me that you would (of, have) driven the car in its present condition.
8. You (sure, surely) are walking (slow, slowly) today.
9. After I lost twenty pounds, all my clothing became very (lose, loose).
10. Try (to, and) find that address so that I can mail this package.
11. I'm (liable, likely) to cry if you keep telling that (real, really) sad story.
12. We do not have to take such abuse (off of, from) you.
13. It's a shame that the train is going so (slow, slowly).
14. Be careful not to (loose, lose) your building permit.
15. (Many, Lots of) people will be visiting our city during the fair.
16. Do you mean that you are (real, really) serious about quitting work?
17. Try (to, and) understand that it is essential for this order to be shipped today.
18. Please don't rush me, for I am (slow, slowly).
19. I would (have, of) been president, but I became too lazy.
20. Juan and Carlos are (seldom, seldom ever) absent from work.
21. The (person, party) you are to meet will be wearing a blue suit.
22. I was very careful as I stepped (off, off of) the bus.
23. If you aren't careful pitching that baseball, you are (liable, likely) to injure your arm.
24. She is (real, really) interested in finding another job.
25. They are now beginning to take the shingles (off, off of) the roof.
26. This (lose, loose) change may wear a hole in my pocket and cause me to (lose, loose) my money and keys.
27. Kim (seldom ever, rarely) becomes irritated during stressful situations.
28. You (sure, surely) finished that piece of cake in record time.
29. That horse would (of, have) thrown me if I had not grabbed the saddle horn with one hand.
30. Isn't it terrible how (slow, slowly) we are moving in this traffic?

Unnecessary Words

The first sentence of each group contains an underlined expression that should not be used. The second sentence is correct.

1. My <u>friend he</u> is the one who made the raft for us.
   My friend is the one who made the raft for us.
2. What will you do with <u>that there</u> pile of leaves?
   What will you do with that pile of leaves?
3. I don't know where to set <u>this here</u> large rosebush.
   I don't know where to set this large rosebush.
4. Do you know where the fire chief <u>is at</u>?
   Do you know where the fire chief is?
5. No one <u>had ought</u> to borrow materials without permission.
   No one ought to (or <u>should</u>) borrow materials without permission.
6. The city manager decided to buy that <u>kind of a</u> parking meter.
   The city manager decided to buy that kind of parking meter.
7. Everyone <u>has got</u> time enough to finish the review pages.
   Everyone has time enough to finish the review pages.
8. The company treasurer <u>went and made</u> a serious mistake in the final tabulation.
   The company treasurer made a serious mistake in the final tabulation.

Practice

Underline the incorrect word or words in the following sentences. Write the correct word or words on the line at the end of each sentence. If the word should be omitted, write *omit* on the line.

1. If you have come for an oar, take that there one. _____

2. My friend Hal he is a fine mechanic. _____

3. The treasurer had ought to give a brief report. _____

4. He went and made those parts without instruction. _____

5. Please don't tell me that there car is yours. _____

6. What kind of a rosebush is this? _____

7. Who went and made this delicious pudding? _____

Review

Underline the correct word in each of these sentences.

1. Juan could not help being (affected, effected) by this sudden popularity.
2. The fashion model walked (in, into) the room and sat down.
3. (Lots of, Many) people visit Michigan and Illinois each year.
4. Must we walk much (further, farther) to reach the river?
5. How (can, may) we decide which television set is the best?
6. Customs today are different (from, than) those of the colonial era.
7. That child is the (cutest, most adorable) one in the pageant.
8. When the pipe (burst, bursted), the basement was completely flooded.
9. Please (accept, except) this token of our love and appreciation.
10. (Its, It's) a shame that the puppy injured (its, it's) foot.
11. (In back of, Behind) the wall stood three disgruntled customers.
12. No one seemed (enthused, enthusiastic) about the new boss.
13. Martin acted (like, as) a dictator who had become drunk with power.
14. I will try (and, to) visit the nursing home each week.
15. Will it be (all right, alright) for us to stand on your lawn to watch the parade?
16. Rose was (awfully, very) disappointed when we could not visit her.
17. The continuous noise (aggravated, irritated) us for over an hour.
18. There were (less, fewer) people present than we had expected.
19. I am sorry that these apples are not (as, so) ripe as those.
20. Melton gave us a (funny, strange) look when he heard our remark.
21. Donna told us that she saw (a, an) enormous mountain lion.
22. Do you feel (bad, badly) today?
23. He has always filled the orders (well, good).
24. The officer warned us to drive (slow, slowly) when the roads are icy.
25. My (brother, brother he) collected coins for years.
26. (This, This here) food is the best I ever tasted.
27. Everyone has gone (except, accept) your mother.
28. Alfredo has (already, all ready) mowed his front yard.
29. Do you mean that you couldn't find them (anywhere, anywheres)?
30. I'm not as smart (like, as) she is.
31. Please stand here (beside, besides) me until the bus arrives.
32. A (bunch, group) of people will meet us at the bowling alley.
33. Stan could (of, have) cleaned his paint brushes.
34. I went to see those original paintings, but I was not (enthused, enthusiastic).
35. Don't expect us to walk much (farther, further) in this heavy rain.

Directions: Choose the correct words. Blacken the numbers to the right that correspond with your choices.

1. This is (a, an) experiment that is (very, awfully) important.
   1   2   3   4   ① ② ③ ④

2. Please (accept, except) my apologies for (lots of, many)
           1   2   3   4

   reasons.   ① ② ③ ④

3. She speaks (slowly, slow), and she (seldom ever, rarely)
               1   2   3   4

   makes an error in grammar.   ① ② ③ ④

4. I am going to try (to, and) (lose, loose) weight this month.   ① ② ③ ④
                      1   2   3   4

5. (Learn, Teach) me the correct way to hold the golf club so
    1   2

   that I can become a (really, real) good player.   ① ② ③ ④
                        3   4

6. Diego is (enthused, enthusiastic) about his job, but he could
            1   2

   (of, have) been very disappointed.   ① ② ③ ④
    3   4

7. (Fewer, Less) people were invited since we have
    1   2

   (fewer, less) space.   ① ② ③ ④
    3   4

8. A (group, bunch) of people were (affected, effected)
      1   2   3   4

   by the layoff.   ① ② ③ ④

9. This argument (among, between) all the members is
                  1   2

   different (from, than) the last argument.   ① ② ③ ④
              3   4

10. We are (all ready, already) to leave if you (can, may)
            1   2   3   4

    make it without us.   ① ② ③ ④

11. You speak (like, as if) you would rather be
               1   2

    (anywhere, anywheres) else than here.   ① ② ③ ④
     3   4

12. When that balloon (burst, bursted), the noise
                       1   2

    (aggravated, irritated) the child.   ① ② ③ ④
     3   4

13. That car (in back of, behind) the van is (likely, liable)
              1   2   3   4

    to be hit.   ① ② ③ ④

Vocabulary and Spelling

Lesson 1 Synonyms

Synonyms are words that have the same or very similar meanings. Synonyms are used to make writing and speaking more interesting. Most dictionaries list synonyms for words. Synonyms can also be studied in a thesaurus.

Practice

Underline two words in each line that are synonyms of the first word.

absurd	kind	foolish	abstract	silly
amateur	novice	professional	orator	beginner
awkward	graceful	moronic	clumsy	inept
comrade	opponent	friend	foe	associate
concentrate	dislike	consolidate	omit	strengthen
delay	expect	recover	wait	detain
demonstrate	show	exhibit	replace	excite
denied	contradicted	accepted	inspired	negated
eager	inferior	avid	enthusiastic	smart
efficient	effective	capable	clumsy	inferior
elevate	exalt	punish	lower	raise
essential	standard	vital	necessary	delicate
feeble	decrepit	infirm	strong	vivacious
freedom	restraint	liberty	independence	power
gloomy	dark	bright	murky	gleaming
hide	expose	confess	conceal	secrete
indignant	angry	happy	careless	irate
interrogate	answer	question	infiltrate	inquire of
interrupt	aid	stop	hinder	sing
pale	pallid	dim	bright	plant
prize	reward	supply	trophy	decorate
shrewd	cunning	sagacious	inhibited	wasteful
visible	apparent	perceptible	concealed	smooth

Lesson II Antonyms

Antonyms are words that are opposite in meaning. Many nouns, adjectives, verbs, and adverbs have antonyms. Dictionaries sometimes list antonyms after the definition for a word. Another source for antonyms is a thesaurus.

Some Common Antonyms

day—night   beautiful—ugly   black—white
happy—sad   live—die   noisy—quiet

Practice

Each numbered word has an antonym either in column **a** or in column **b**. Match each numbered word to its antonym by writing the number in the blank.

a

1. help   _____ dirty
2. cool   _____ believe
3. sold   _____ debit
4. dull   _____ narrow
5. clean   _____ wasteful
6. lead   _____ prosperity
7. straight   _____ present
8. high   _____ hinder
9. lose   _____ find
10. admit   _____ shrink
11. adversity _____ follow
12. credit   _____ full
13. advance   _____ bought
14. vague   _____ crooked
15. absent   _____ scarce
16. thrifty   _____ deny

b

17. stretch   _____ sweet
18. plentiful _____ retreat
19. doubt   _____ alive
20. end   _____ warm
21. add   _____ cramped
22. free   _____ common
23. good   _____ pleasure
24. rough   _____ kind
25. spacious   _____ subtract
26. mean   _____ evil
27. pain   _____ smooth
28. unique   _____ confined
29. empty   _____ sharp
30. bitter   _____ clear
31. dead   _____ begin
32. wide   _____ low

Lesson III Homonyms and Spelling Rules

Homonyms are words pronounced alike but spelled and defined differently. In speaking, an error in the use of these words is not evident; in writing, the words do cause spelling problems for many people. Learn the meaning and spelling of each word that is unfamiliar to you.

air, heir
allowed, aloud
altar, alter
bare, bear
baring, bearing
beach, beech
berth, birth
blew, blue
board, bored
brake, break
bridal, bridle
canvas, canvass
ceiling, sealing
cite, sight, site
clause, claws
coarse, course
complement, compliment
dear, deer
dew, due, do
dyeing, dying
fair, fare
flair, flare
flew, flue, flu
for, fore, four

forth, fourth
grate, great
hair, hare
heal, heel
hear, here
heard, herd
hole, whole
idle, idol
it's, its
knew, new
lessen, lesson
main, mane
might, mite
one, won
pair, pare, pear
passed, past
peace, piece
plain, plane
plum, plumb
principal, principle
rain, reign, rein
read, reed
read, red
real, reel

right, rite, write
road, rode
root, route
sale, sail
sea, see
seam, seem
shone, shown
side, sighed
soar, sore
some, sum
stake, steak
stationary, stationery
steal, steel
straight, strait
their, there, they're
threw, through
to, too, two
vain, vane, vein
wait, weight
ware, wear, where
wave, waive
weak, week
whose, who's
yoke, yolk

Practice 1

Mark out the incorrect word or words in each sentence.

1. We plan to spend a (week, weak) in Colorado.
2. Our (won, one) victory is the (one, won) that we (one, won) today.
3. At the (fare, fair) we could (see, sea) (some, sum) (knew, new) machines.
4. Martha (side, sighed) as the (plane, plain) (flew, flu) out of (sight, site).
5. The (clause, claws) of the tiger ripped (through, threw) the (canvas, canvass).
6. The (deer, dear) led her fawns over the familiar (coarse, course).
7. He was (air, heir) (to, two, too) a (great, grate) fortune.

8. This is the (cite, site, sight) for the new building.
9. May I (complement, compliment) those (who's, whose) work made this possible.
10. The (male, mail) for this (root, route) is (dew, due) now, but (it's, its) late.
11. Have I (shown, shone) you the lovely (stationary, stationery)?
12. With (bare, bear) hands the Incas climbed (there, their) (way, weigh) to the (alter, altar).
13. The (principal, principle) event will be held in the tent.
14. The (seam, seem) in the stocking (seams, seems) to be crooked.
15. Do you consider this (plain, plane) (fair, fare) to be (fair, fare)?

I Before E Spelling Rule

Write *i* before *e* except after *c*, or where sounded as *a* in *neighbor* and *weigh*. Unfortunately, this basic rule has a number of exceptions, some of which are listed below.

ancient	foreign	leisure	society
counterfeit	forfeit	neither	species
efficient	height	science	their
either	heir	seize	weird

Practice 2

In each group of words, one word may be misspelled. If one is misspelled, write the letter beside the word on the line at the right. If no words are misspelled, write **d** on the line.

1. (a) anceint   (b) belief   (c) chief   (d) none   _____

2. (a) counterfeit   (b) believe   (c) pateince   (d) none   _____

3. (a) brief   (b) efficeint   (c) friend   (d) none   _____

4. (a) piece   (b) either   (c) deciet   (d) none   _____

5. (a) hygiene   (b) conceit   (c) foriegn   (d) none   _____

6. (a) forfeit   (b) height   (c) niece   (d) none   _____

7. (a) peir   (b) heir   (c) leisure   (d) none   _____

8. (a) neither   (b) science   (c) experience   (d) none   _____

9. (a) conceit   (b) sieze   (c) view   (d) none   _____

10. (a) society   (b) their   (c) wierd   (d) none   _____

11. (a) pierce   (b) cieling   (c) cashier   (d) none   _____

12. (a) species   (b) experience   (c) piece   (d) none   _____

13. (a) field   (b) concieve   (c) deceive   (d) none   _____

14. (a) feirce   (b) lieutenant   (c) neighbor   (d) none   _____

More Useful Spelling Rules

■ In most instances, if a word ends in -e, drop the e to add a suffix that begins with a vowel. Keep the e if the suffix begins with a consonant.

move + ing = moving   move + ment = movement

■ The suffix -s can be added to most nouns and verbs. However, if a word ends in -s, -ss, -sh, -ch, -x, or -zz, the suffix -es is added.

loss—losses   lunch—lunches   push—pushes
flex—flexes   fox—foxes   buzz—buzzes

■ If a word with stress on the last syllable ends in a consonant preceded by a vowel, double the last consonant to add a suffix that begins with a vowel.

mad—madder   refer—referring   *but* travel—traveling

■ If a word ends in -y preceded by a consonant, change the y to i to add a suffix, unless the suffix begins with i.

beauty—beautiful   lady—ladies   reply—replying

■ If a word ends in -y preceded by a vowel, keep the y when adding a suffix.

relay—relaying   play—playing   delay—delayed

■ If a word ends in a single -f or in -fe, the f or fe usually is changed to a v before adding the suffix -es.

wolf—wolves   life—lives   half—halves

Practice 3

Mark out the incorrect word or words in each sentence.

1. We were slowly (moveing, moving) since the start of the program had been (delayed, delaid) for an hour.
2. Those three (boxs, boxes) that contained our (lunches, lunchs) had been (beautyfully, beautifully) decorated.
3. They are now (replaing, replaying) the fantastic run that was made by the quarterback.
4. That candidate has received the (endorsment, endorsement) of a number of political leaders in our state.
5. These (loafs, loaves) of bread are too stale to eat.
6. The hockey team has had three straight (loss's, losses), and I am (begining, beginning) to doubt that it will win a game all season.

Answer the following questions.

1. If a word ends in a single -f or in -fe, what must you do to add -es?

   _____

   _____

2. When do you double the final consonant of a word before adding a suffix?

   _____

   _____

3. When is the y at the end of a word changed to i before adding a suffix?

   _____

   _____

4. When is the y at the end of a word not changed to i before adding a suffix?

   _____

   _____

5. When is the e at the end of a word dropped before adding a suffix?

   _____

   _____

A Spelling List

You should be able to spell all the words in the following spelling list. Study the list and learn the spellings and meanings of any words that are not familiar to you.

absence	appreciate	campaign	constitution
accelerator	asthma	cancel	contagious
accept	astronaut	candidate	cough
accident	athletics	carburetor	courteous
accommodate	atmosphere	career	courtesy
accountant	axle	catalog	credit
accurate	battery	certificate	creditor
acquaintance	beautiful	character	criticism
acre	beneficiary	chimney	curtain
address	bicycle	chisel	customer
advice	biscuit	choir	defense
against	blouse	circuit	definitely
alien	bologna	citizenship	democracy
all right	brake	clutch	deposit
almost	breathe	cocoa	depot
aluminum	broccoli	column	depth
annual	budget	commission	description
answer	bureau	committee	desperate
antenna	business	comparatively	develop
antique	cabinet	concrete	dictionary
anxious	cafeteria	conquer	disappointment

discipline
disease
dissatisfied
dividend
doesn't
dutiful
earnest
eighth
elevator
embarrass
endeavor
equator
especially
excellent
exercise
familiar
fatigue
faucet
February
forty
fourth
garage
gasoline
genuine
government
graph
guarantee
guardian
guilty
gymnasium
half
hammer
hemisphere
humorous
ignition
imitation
immediately
income
influence
initial
installment
interest
inventory
island

judgment
justice
khaki
knob
knowledge
laboratory
lawyer
license
lightning
loneliness
losing
loving
lubricate
lying
making
maple
marriage
mattress
mayonnaise
mayor
meant
medicine
mirror
monotonous
mortgage
muffler
municipal
musician
necessarily
necessary
negotiable
ninety
ninth
nuclear
nuisance
occurred
opinion
opportunity
organize
original
overtime
ocean
occasionally
occupation

parallel
particularly
perhaps
personnel
picnic
pilot
piston
pleasant
plumbing
pneumonia
policy
possess
possibility
practice
prejudice
privilege
probate
procedure
professor
puncture
purpose
quite
radiator
realize
recognize
reference
refrigerator
repetition
representative
restaurant
rheumatism
rhythm
safety
salary
sandwich
satisfactory
scent
schedule
scissors
separate
shovel
siege
similar
sincerely

spaghetti
straight
suede
suggestion
superintendent
superior
surgeon
surprise
sympathy
syrup
television
temperament
tendency
thorough
tobacco
traffic
tragedy
transferred
transmission
truly
Tuesday
twelfth
umbrella
using
usual
vacation
vacuum
vicinity
vitamin
waist
warranty
waste
Wednesday
where
whether
whole
woman
would
wrap
writing
written
wrote

Adapted from *Gateways to Correct Spelling,* Revised Edition, by Fred C. Ayer, Steck-Vaughn Company, Austin, Texas.

In each group of words, one word may be misspelled. If one is misspelled, write the letter beside the word on the line at the right. If no words are mispelled, write **d** on the line.

1. (a) ambarass (b) license (c) develop (d) none _____
2. (a) guilty (b) whether (c) ninety (d) none _____
3. (a) business (b) chimney (c) schedule (d) none _____
4. (a) sincerly (b) sandwich (c) truly (d) none _____
5. (a) valient (b) organize (c) genius (d) none _____
6. (a) breathe (b) disease (c) occurred (d) none _____
7. (a) making (b) familiar (c) loseing (d) none _____
8. (a) peirce (b) recognize (c) receive (d) none _____
9. (a) canidate (b) opinion (c) deceive (d) none _____
10. (a) dictionary (b) height (c) judgment (d) none _____
11. (a) paralel (b) scent (c) ninth (d) none _____
12. (a) guarantee (b) cough (c) Tuesday (d) none _____
13. (a) weird (b) useing (c) twelfth (d) none _____
14. (a) knowledge (b) endeavor (c) tobaco (d) none _____
15. (a) column (b) perhaps (c) eighth (d) none _____
16. (a) similar (b) vacumm (c) vicinity (d) none _____
17. (a) imitation (b) initial (c) omitted (d) none _____
18. (a) seige (b) interest (c) sincerely (d) none _____
19. (a) discipline (b) dutiful (c) wolfs (d) none _____
20. (a) dissatisfied (b) efficient (c) genuine (d) none _____
21. (a) character (b) absence (c) fourth (d) none _____
22. (a) municipal (b) courtesy (c) allmost (d) none _____
23. (a) humorous (b) surgeon (c) lonelyness (d) none _____
24. (a) superior (b) anual (c) musician (d) none _____
25. (a) corteous (b) influence (c) cafeteria (d) none _____
26. (a) campaine (b) island (c) orchestra (d) none _____
27. (a) refering (b) quarrel (c) lying (d) none _____
28. (a) original (b) lightning (c) restaurant (d) none _____
29. (a) privilege (b) medicine (c) comittee (d) none _____
30. (a) earnest (b) posess (c) piston (d) none _____
31. (a) guardian (b) ritten (c) criticism (d) none _____
32. (a) personally (b) variety (c) wrap (d) none _____
33. (a) picknic (b) scissors (c) pleasant (d) none _____
34. (a) bureau (b) achievement (c) athletics (d) none _____

Directions: Choose the correct words. Blacken the numbers to the right that correspond with your choices.

1. A synonym of *hide* is (confess, conceal); a synonym of *pale*
   ₁   ₂

   is (dim, bucket).   ① ② ③ ④
      ₃   ₄

2. An antonym of *spacious* is (spectacular, cramped);
   ₁   ₂

   an antonym of *thrifty* is (wasteful, prosperous).   ① ② ③ ④
                          ₃   ₄

3. The (air, heir) to the fortune will be (hear, here) tomorrow.   ① ② ③ ④
      ₁ ₂   ₃   ₄

4. That car was on the (right, write) side of the (rode, road).   ① ② ③ ④
                       ₁   ₂   ₃   ₄

5. This (stationary, stationery) is pretty, but I think I'll just
        ₁   ₂

   write a note on this (piece, peace) of paper.   ① ② ③ ④
                        ₃   ₄

6. The (site, sight) for this building is (grate, great)!   ① ② ③ ④
      ₁   ₂   ₃   ₄

7. We (road, rode) for several hours in the (rain, rein).   ① ② ③ ④
      ₁   ₂   ₃   ₄

8. This (leisure, liesure) suit really looks (weird, wierd).   ① ② ③ ④
        ₁   ₂   ₃   ₄

9. That is one (foreign, foriegn) government we can count on
              ₁   ₂

   as being a (friend, freind).   ① ② ③ ④
              ₃   ₄

10. She is (mader, madder) than either of the other two
           ₁   ₂

    (ladys, ladies).   ① ② ③ ④
     ₃   ₄

11. We were frightened for our (lifes, lives) when the
                               ₁   ₂

    (wolves, wolfs) started to howl.   ① ② ③ ④
     ₃   ₄

12. That (maple, mapel) tree is the largest in our
         ₁   ₂

    (visinity, vicinity).   ① ② ③ ④
     ₃   ₄

13. The new (restaurant, restarant) has a (variaty, variety)
            ₁   ₂   ₃   ₄

    of fine foods.   ① ② ③ ④

14. Did you say the (acselerater, accelerator) is
                    ₁   ₂

    (almost, allmost) broken?   ① ② ③ ④
     ₃   ₄

15. The bird (flu, flew) (passed, past) our house
             ₁ ₂   ₃   ₄

    a few minutes ago.   ① ② ③ ④

Name: _____

Date: _____ Score: _____

A. Indicate whether each sentence is complete, incomplete, simple, or complex by blackening the space to the right having the same number as the correct answer you have chosen.

1. Kay and Roy wanted to go on a nice summer vacation.   ① ② ③ ④ ⑤
   (1) complete, complex   (4) incomplete
   (2) simple, complex   (5) incomplete, simple
   (3) complete, simple

2. Looking on with horror, the two girls saw the tornado approaching.   ① ② ③ ④ ⑤
   (1) complete, simple   (4) complete, complex
   (2) incomplete   (5) incomplete, simple
   (3) incomplete, complex

3. If I had intended to buy the car.   ① ② ③ ④ ⑤
   (1) incomplete, simple   (4) complete, complex
   (2) complete, simple   (5) incomplete
   (3) simple, complex

B. Check the underlined part of each sentence. If the underlined part is incorrect, blacken the space to the right having the same number as the correct answer you have chosen. If there is no error, mark answer space 5.

1. The <u>sazukis are wealthy now; but</u> we knew them before they struck oil.   ① ② ③ ④ ⑤
   (1) Sazukis are wealthy now: but
   (2) sazukis are wealthy now, but
   (3) sazukis are wealthy now. But
   (4) Sazukis are wealthy now, but
   (5) no error

2. Your <u>nurse, who is a very kind person, came</u> to check on you several times.   ① ② ③ ④ ⑤
   (1) Nurse, who is a very kind person, came
   (2) nurse; who is a very kind person, came
   (3) nurse: who is a very kind person, came
   (4) nurse who is a very kind person came
   (5) no error

3. Isn't it very cold in the <u>scandinavian countries during the winter.</u>   ① ② ③ ④ ⑤
   (1) Scandinavian Countries during the winter.
   (2) Scandinavian countries during the winter.
   (3) Scandinavian countries during the Winter?
   (4) Scandinavian countries during the winter?
   (5) no error

4. When we move to <u>the south we will live in birmingham, alabama.</u>   ① ② ③ ④ ⑤
   (1) the South we will live in Birmingham, alabama
   (2) the South, we will live in Birmingham, Alabama
   (3) the South; we will live in Birmingham, Alabama
   (4) the south, we will live in Birmingham, Alabama
   (5) no error

5. That <u>indian leader spoke at the United nations</u> yesterday.   ① ② ③ ④ ⑤
   (1) indian leader spoke at the united nations
   (2) indian leader spoke at the united Nations
   (3) Indian leader spoke at the United Nations
   (4) Indian Leader spoke at the United Nations
   (5) no error

6. Your <u>statement I must admit really shocked me James.</u>   ① ② ③ ④ ⑤
   (1) statement I must admit really shocked, me, James
   (2) statement, I must admit really shocked me James
   (3) statement, I must admit, really shocked me James
   (4) statement, I must admit, really shocked me, James
   (5) no error

7. This <u>job—a really fine position—means a move to detroit, michigan.</u>   ① ② ③ ④ ⑤
   (1) job—a really fine position—means a move to Detroit, Michigan.
   (2) Job, a really fine position—means a move to Detroit, Michigan.
   (3) job, a really fine position, means a move to Detroit, Michigan.
   (4) job, a really fine position, means a move to Detroit, michigan?
   (5) no error

8. "Move this rock," said Jan, "and I will plant some grass seeds." ① ② ③ ④ ⑤

(1) "Move this rock, said Jan, and I will plant some grass seeds."

(2) "Move this rock," said Jan, and I will plant some grass seeds "

(3) "Move this rock, said Jan, "and I will plant some grass seeds."

(4) Move this rock, said Jan, and I will plant some grass seeds "

(5) no error

9. The song "My Wild irish rose was sung by the tenor. ① ② ③ ④ ⑤

(1) song, "My Wild Irish Rose," was

(2) song My Wild Irish Rose was

(3) song—"My Wild Irish Rose" was

(4) Song, "My Wild Irish Rose," was

(5) no error

10. That answer—needless to say, the wrong answer, was funny. ① ② ③ ④ ⑤

(1) answer, needless to say the wrong answer, was

(2) answer—needless to say, the wrong answer—was

(3) answer: needless to say, the wrong answer, was

(4) answer; needless to say, the wrong answer, was

(5) no error

C. Choose the correct words. Blacken the numbers to the right that correspond to the words you select.

1. The (babys, babies) were playing with several (tois, toys). ① ② ③ ④
   1   2   3   4

2. Those (potatoes, potatos) are so tough we can hardly cut
   1   2
   them with our (knifes, knives). ① ② ③ ④
                  3   4

3. There were six (deer, deers) eating food from the
   1   2
   (boxies, boxes). ① ② ③ ④
   3   4

4. Both (mothers-in-law, mother-in-laws) agreed to stay with
   1   2
   the (childs, children). ① ② ③ ④
   3   4

5. (Garza's and Smith's, Garza and Smith's) Hardware Store
   1   2
   is my (aunt's, aunts) favorite store. ① ② ③ ④
   3   4

6. It was (her, she) (who, whom) I called yesterday. ① ② ③ ④
   1   2   3   4

7. Juan and (her, she) say that the time card is (her's, hers). ① ② ③ ④
   1   2   3   4

8. Don't tell me you are afraid of (him, his) riding with
   1   2
   (I, me). ① ② ③ ④
   3   4

119

9. The cars waited for us, Stan and (me, I), to cross, but
   1   2
   (him and me, he and I) could not hurry.
   3   4
   ① ② ③ ④

10. Did (her and him, she and he) send (Sandy and me,
    1   2   3
    Sandy and I) this candy?
    4
    ① ② ③ ④

11. A colon should be used after the salutation of a (business,
    1
    friendly) letter and before a (list, break in thought).
    2   3   4
    ① ② ③ ④

12. Juan is the person (who, which) called Nora and (I, me).
    1   2   3   4
    ① ② ③ ④

13. I normally speak politely to (whoever, whomever) I meet,
    1   2
    but I must admit that I was not courteous to (him, he).
    3   4
    ① ② ③ ④

14. (This, That) vase by the door was a gift from Larry and
    1   2
    (she, her).
    3   4
    ① ② ③ ④

15. Someone in those trees (is, are) calling to the dog Mary
    1   2
    and (I, me) saw.
    3   4
    ① ② ③ ④

16. He saw (himself, hisself) in a mirror as (ourselves, we)
    1   2   3   4
    walked through the deserted house.
    ① ② ③ ④

17. It was Shirley and (I, me) (who, whom) you saw in the
    1   2   3   4
    garden.
    ① ② ③ ④

18. Each is to fix (his, their) own sandwich, for several of
    1   2
    them (do, does) not like the way I fix sandwiches.
    3   4
    ① ② ③ ④

19. That glass was (broke, broken) after I had (drunk, drank)
    1   2   3   4
    the cola.
    ① ② ③ ④

20. That rug was (thrown, throwed) from a pickup, and our
    1   2
    dog (drug, dragged) it into the yard.
    3   4
    ① ② ③ ④

21. Has the band (begun, began) to play? I have (forgotten,
    1   2   3
    forgot) what time the concert is to begin.
    4
    ① ② ③ ④

22. Yesterday I (lay, laid) in the sun too long; today I will
    1   2
    (lie, lay) outside for only a few minutes.
    3   4
    ① ② ③ ④

23. The group of volunteers (is, are) standing quietly waiting
    1   2
    to be (chose, chosen).
    3   4
    ① ② ③ ④

24. (Was, Were) you late due to carelessness, or (is, are) there
    1   2   3   4
    good reasons for it?
    ① ② ③ ④

25. Either one of the Smiths or Mr. Brewster (is, are) driving,
    1   2
    for neither Barry nor she (want, wants) to drive in this
    3   4
    traffic.
    ① ② ③ ④

120

26. (Whose, Who's) coat was left? (It's, Its) a very
    1   2   3   4

    attractive one.   ① ② ③ ④

27. He (don't, doesn't) think (their, they're) ready to leave.   ① ② ③ ④
        1   2   3   4

28. (Your, You're) photograph is great; (its, it's) too bad the
    1   2   3   4

    negative was lost.   ① ② ③ ④

29. She seems (sader, sadder), but she accepted the bad news
              1   2

    (more easier, more easily) than I thought she would.   ① ② ③ ④
     3   4

30. Move (slowly, slow); I (can't, can) hardly see the path.   ① ② ③ ④
         1   2   3   4

31. I don't need (no, any) bad advice; good advice is (usefuller,
                 1   2   3

    more useful).   ① ② ③ ④
    4

32. Who is the (lazier, laziest) person at work, and who can
                1   2

    work the (faster, fastest)?   ① ② ③ ④
             3   4

33. A subordinate conjunction joins the (dependent, independent)
                                         1   2

    clause to the (dependent, independent) clause.   ① ② ③ ④
                   3   4

34. Prepositions show a relationship between a (noun, verb) or
                                               1   2

    (adjective, pronoun) object and some other word in the
     3   4

    sentence.   ① ② ③ ④

35. Please (accept, except) my apologies, for I am
           1   2

    (very, awfully) sorry.   ① ② ③ ④
     3   4

36. That food was cooked (bad, badly), and all of us feel
                         1   2

    (bad, badly) today.   ① ② ③ ④
     3   4

37. Sandra walked (among, between) the many rose bushes,
                  1   2

    and she was (enthusiastic, enthused) about the quality of
                 3   4

    the blossoms.   ① ② ③ ④

38. Let's follow this path a little (farther, further), for we are
                                    1   2

    (likely, liable) to get lost if we leave it.   ① ② ③ ④
     3   4

39. Which of the following word pairs are adjectives?
    (mail, cool) (bright, cool) (since, durable) (genuine, sad)   ① ② ③ ④
    1   2   3   4

40. Which of the following word pairs are adverbs?
    (very, coolly) (beautiful, correctly) (soon, hardly) (happily, tall)   ① ② ③ ④
    1   2   3   4

41. She said that she was (real, really) sorry that you don't
                          1   2

    feel (good, well).   ① ② ③ ④
         3   4

42. There are (less, fewer) people than we thought standing
              1   2

    (behind, in back of) the screen.   ① ② ③ ④
     3   4

43. Never step (off of, off) the curb without looking, for you
    1   2
    might step (in, into) a puddle.
              3   4   ① ② ③ ④

44. That dog (seldom ever, rarely) barks, and I (sure, surely)
            1   2   3   4
    am glad.   ① ② ③ ④

45. This outlet comes (strait, straight) from the (mane, main) line.   ① ② ③ ④
                      1   2   3   4

46. (Try and, Try to) start the car again; (its, it's) battery is
    1   2   3   4
    just weak.   ① ② ③ ④

47. (That, That there) memo (had ought, should) be sent to
    1   2   3   4
    the boss.   ① ② ③ ④

48. A synonym for *sad* is (weary, unhappy); an antonym for
                          1   2
    absent is (present, vague).   ① ② ③ ④
                3   4

49. Let me (compliment, complement) you on your work; the
           1   2
    (whole, hole) department knows how well you have done.   ① ② ③ ④
     3   4

50. I didn't mean to (embarass, embarrass) you when I
                     1   2
    mentioned your bad (coff, cough).   ① ② ③ ④
                        3   4

51. That (chimney, chimley) is leaning, and it is a real
         1   2
    (safty, safety) hazard.   ① ② ③ ④
     3   4

52. My grandmother is (ninty, ninety) years old, and one of
                      1   2
    her (nieghbors, neighbors) is almost one hundred years old.   ① ② ③ ④
         3   4

53. (Wednesday, Wendsday) we will have to (rap, wrap)
    1   2   3   4
    the presents.   ① ② ③ ④

54. The supervisor will be giving (achievement, acheivement)
                                  1   2
    awards, not (critisism, criticism).   ① ② ③ ④
                 3   4

55. You gave me good (advise, advice), and I (definitely,
                     1   2   3
    definitly) plan to follow it.   ① ② ③ ④
    4

56. The couple had to put down (ernest, earnest) money to
                               1   2
    keep from (loosing, losing) the house they want to buy.   ① ② ③ ④
               3   4

57. That (morgage, mortgage) is (quite, quiet) large.   ① ② ③ ④
         1   2   3   4

58. A synonym for *indignant* is (undignified, irate);
                                 1   2
    an antonym for *vivacious* is (spiritless, energetic).   ① ② ③ ④
                                  3   4

59. I think I'll just eat a small (piece, peace) of (steak, stake).   ① ② ③ ④
                                  1   2   3   4

60. We were (two, too) (vane, vain) to admit our mistakes.   ① ② ③ ④
            1   2   3   4

61. The weather reporter said that (rain, rein) is (dew, due)
                                   1   2   3   4
    tonight.   ① ② ③ ④

62. That (pare, pair) of shoes is now on (sail, sale).
        1   2   3   4   ① ② ③ ④

63. Your new (stationary, stationery) is attractive; I (might,
                1   2   3

mite) buy some, too.   ① ② ③ ④
4

64. I (beleive, believe) that we should (cancel, cansel) our
  1   2   3   4

reservation.   ① ② ③ ④

65. Who voted (aginst, against) this new (policy, polisy)
            1   2   3   4

change?   ① ② ③ ④

66. Did you (alter, altar) your memo to the (personel,
        1   2   3

personnel) department?   ① ② ③ ④
4

67. The (hole, whole) squadron was (truely, truly) frightened. ① ② ③ ④
    1   2   3   4

68. Do you (sincerly, sincerely) (believe, beleive) you are
       1   2   3   4

correct?   ① ② ③ ④

69. (There, Their) is where (their, they're) going to build. ① ② ③ ④
   1   2   3   4

70. We just walked (passed, past) the (main, mane) building. ① ② ③ ④
            1   2   3   4

71. There were (four, fore) (dear, deer) grazing in that pasture. ① ② ③ ④
          1   2   3   4

72. I (see, sea) that someone (road, rode) the black horse
   1   2   3   4

today.   ① ② ③ ④

73. The car sped along the (rode, road) and went (threw,
                      1   2   3

through) the tunnel.   ① ② ③ ④
4

74. Did you eat the (plum, plumb) and the (pear, pare)?   ① ② ③ ④
               1   2   3   4

D. Write each sentence correctly by adding all needed capital letters and marks of punctuation.

1. this painting said lupe will be auctioned next week _____

   _____

2. jim werent you in new york on december 24 1984 _____

   _____

3. you should meet us within the hour or we will be too late _____

   _____

4. after we change the oil in the car we will shop for groceries _____

   _____

5. that dog an unusually friendly animal belongs to carlos said jean _____

   _____

123

Mastery Test Correlation Chart

Some multi-part items measure different content areas. In these cases, the page numbers suggested for review are separated by an asterisk(*). When a number after an asterisk is lower than the page numbers preceding it, this reflects the order of the content covered in the sentence.

For any item(s) you miss on the Mastery Test, use this chart to find on which page(s) review can be found.

Mastery Test Item #	Review Page(s)	Mastery Test Item #	Review Page(s)	Mastery Test Item #	Review Page(s)
A. 1	8, 12, 15	22	29	56	114
2	8, 12, 15	23	30-31	57	114
3	8, 12, 15	24	30-31	58	108-109
		25	30-31	59	110
B. 1	88-89 * 78	26	32 * 101	60	110
2	78	27	30-31	61	110
3	88-89 * 9, 77	28	32 * 101	62	110
4	88-89 * 78	29	68-69	63	110
5	88	30	66	64	111, 113
6	79-80	31	65 * 68-69	65	113-114
7	78 * 83 * 88-89	32	68-69	66	110 * 114
8	84-85	33	73	67	110 * 114
9	80 * 86 * 88	34	72	68	114 * 111
10	83	35	94-95 * 97	69	57 * 110
		36	97	70	110
C. 1	37-38	37	95 * 99-100	71	110
2	37-38	38	101-102 *	72	110
3	37-38		103-104	73	110
4	37-38	39	65	74	110
5	40	40	66		
6	49-50 * 54-55	41	103 * 101	D. 1	84 * 9 * 88 * 77
7	49-50 * 51	42	101	2	9, 89 * 79 * 32 * 88 * 81 * 77
8	49-50	43	103 * 101	3	9, 89 * 12, 78 * 77
9	49-50	44	103	4	9, 89 * 78 * 77
10	49-50	45	114 * 110	5	84 * 9, 89 * 78 * 77
11	82	46	32, 101 * 103		
12	55 * 50	47	57		
13	54 * 50	48	108-109		
14	54 * 50-51	49	110		
15	20 * 50, 61-62	50	113-114		
16	61 * 50	51	113-114		
17	50 * 55	52	114 * 111		
18	51 * 30-31	53	114 * 110		
19	26-28	54	111 * 113		
20	26-28	55	113		
21	26-28				

HANDBOOK

This handbook contains definitions of the terms used in the Worktext®. An example is given with each definition so that the terms may be more easily understood. The definitions are followed by a restatement of the rules found in the book. Although this may seem repetitious, it will be an easy reference source to aid in helping you to become familiar with each term and to feel more at ease with the work.

Contents

Definitions

Adjective. An adjective modifies a noun or a pronoun.

The little puppy was happy.

Adverb. An adverb modifies a verb, an adjective, or another adverb.

She ran very swiftly.

Agreement. Agreement is conformity between two parts of speech in number and in person. Agreement is particularly important with subjects and verbs, as well as with pronouns and their antecedents.

The man with the dogs was Tim.

Antecedent. An antecedent is a noun or a pronoun to which a pronoun refers.

Tell Sue that Helen will come for her.

Antonym. Antonyms are words that are opposite in meaning.

The days were warm, but the nights were cool.

Appositive. An appositive is a word or a group of words that renames a person or a thing that has already been introduced.

The only guest, Mr. Davis, sat near Father.

Clause. A clause is a group of related words containing a subject and a predicate.

All who needed safety goggles were sent to the storeroom.

Collective Noun. A collective noun refers to a group or a collection of people or things that are considered as one unit.

The team shouted with joy.

Comma Blunder. A comma blunder is an error made when two independent clauses are joined by a comma without a coordinating conjunction.

The horse walked slowly its head was bent low.

Common Noun. A noun that names general classes of persons, places, things, concepts, actions, and qualities.

The child stood on the box.

Complex Sentence. A complex sentence contains one independent clause and one or more dependent clauses.

I know (who you are).

125

Compound-Complex Sentence. A compound-complex sentence is composed of two or more independent clauses and one or more dependent clauses.

I know (what you want to know), but I will not answer your questions.

Compound Personal Pronoun. A compound personal pronoun is a pronoun combined with either the suffix *-self* or *-selves.*

I can do the work <u>myself</u>.

Compound Predicate. A predicate composed of two or more predicate verbs is a compound predicate.

The audience <u>laughed</u> and <u>applauded</u>.

Compound Predicate Nominative. A compound predicate nominative is composed of two or more nouns or pronouns that complete a being verb and refer to the subject.

The winners were <u>Mary</u> and <u>I</u>.

Compound Pronoun. A compound pronoun is a pronoun used with one of the following suffixes: *-self, -selves, -ever, -soever.*

Speak to <u>whomever</u> you meet.

Compound Sentence. A compound sentence is formed when two or more independent clauses are joined together.

<u>He needed three nails</u>, but <u>I could find only two</u>.

Compound Subject. A subject composed of nouns or pronouns joined by a conjunction is a compound subject.

The <u>roses</u> and <u>lilies</u> were blooming.

Compound Word. A compound word is composed of two or more words used as one.

Our city is the <u>gateway</u> to Florida.

Conjunction. A conjunction is a word used to connect words, phrases, or clauses.

She <u>and</u> I are friends.

Conjunctive Adverb. A conjunctive adverb is a conjunction used between independent clauses.

I will come; <u>however</u>, I must leave early.

Correlative Conjunction. A correlative conjunction connects words, phrases, or clauses as other conjunctions do; but these conjunctions are used in pairs.

<u>Either</u> the cow <u>or</u> the horse will be put into that pasture.

Declarative Sentence. A declarative sentence makes a statement.

This house is very beautiful.

Demonstrative Pronoun. A demonstrative pronoun is a pronoun that points out.

<u>This</u> is my new car.

Dependent Clause. A dependent clause is a clause that must be used with an independent clause if its meaning is to be clear.

(As he came nearer), I saw the twinkle in his eyes.

Direct Address. Direct address is the use of a person's name, nickname, or another identifying word when speaking to the person.

Wait here, <u>Melda</u>, until I return.

Direct Object. A direct object is the noun or the pronoun that receives the action of a verb.

I wrote the <u>letter</u> yesterday.

Direct Quotation. A direct quotation states the exact words of a speaker.

"The election will be on Tuesday," said Nelson.

Exclamatory Sentence. An exclamatory sentence shows strong feeling.

Move quickly!

Future Tense. The future tense denotes a future time. *Will* or *shall* is used with the present tense of a verb to form the future.

I will go tomorrow.

Gerund. A gerund is an *-ing* form of a verb that is used as a noun.

Fishing is not my favorite sport.

Helping Verb. A helping verb is a verb that helps to form a verb phrase.

The stranger was speaking to me.

Imperative Sentence. An imperative sentence gives a command or states a request.

Come with us to the movie.

Indefinite Pronoun. An indefinite pronoun does not refer to a definite antecedent.

Someone did the work for us.

Independent Clause. An independent clause states the main thought of a sentence and is complete within itself.

When the snow falls, the birds find little food.

Independent Element. An independent element is a word or an expression that has no grammatical connection with the sentence.

Really! That cannot be true!

Indirect Object. An indirect object names the person to or for whom something is done.

I brought Brad the evening paper.

Indirect Quotation. An indirect quotation carries the meaning of a speaker's words, but the exact words are not repeated.

Hal said that he wanted to see me.

Intensive Pronoun. An intensive pronoun, a personal pronoun combined with the suffix *-self* or *-selves,* is used to intensify or to emphasize the noun or pronoun to which it refers.

I myself will speak to her.

Interjection. An interjection is a word or expression that expresses strong or sudden feeling.

Hurry! We are late!

Interrogative Adverb. An interrogative adverb introduces a question.

Where is your chairperson?

Interrogative Sentence. An interrogative sentence asks a question.

Why have you been gone so long?

Irregular Verb. An irregular verb forms its tenses in some other way than by adding *-ed, -d,* or *-t* to the present tense.

Sing as you have never sung before.

Linking Verb. A linking verb (being verb) joins the subject and subject complement.

The message was short. It was she.

Negative Adverb. A negative adverb is an adverb that denies or contradicts.

I never expected to see you again.

Noun. A noun is the name of a person, place, or thing.

The top of the cathedral was covered with glittering gold.

Noun Clause. A noun clause is a dependent clause used as a noun.

I know who the speaker is.
[direct object over "who the speaker"]

Object of a Preposition. The object of a preposition is the noun or the pronoun that completes the prepositional phrase.

She spoke (of her homeland) (to all) (of us).

Parenthetical Expression. A parenthetical expression is a word or a group of words inserted independently into a sentence.

I will, I think, try again for the office.

Personal Pronoun. A personal pronoun denotes the speaker, the person spoken to, or the person spoken of.

I will introduce him to you.

Phrase. A phrase is a group of related words that does not have a subject and a predicate.

Suddenly breaking into a run, she was able to catch me.

Possessive. The possessive form of a word shows ownership.

That couple's house is their most valued possession.

Predicate. The predicate is the part of a sentence that tells something about the subject.

Everyone should study the policies of our democracy.

Predicate Adjective. A predicate adjective follows a being verb and describes the noun or pronoun subject.

South American countries are interesting.

Predicate Nominative. A predicate nominative is a noun or pronoun that follows a being verb and renames the subject.

The rancher was the owner of many acres of land.

Preposition. A preposition is a word that shows the relationship between its object noun or pronoun and some other word in the sentence.

The book (on the desk) tells (about Asia).

Prepositional Phrase. A prepositional phrase is composed of a preposition, its object, and all object modifiers.

Sit down (on the lid) (of my trunk).

Pronoun. A pronoun is a word that takes the place of a noun.

Put it beside those that you brought.

Proper Adjective. A proper adjective is an adjective derived from a proper noun.

The African countries were visited by American politicians.

Proper Noun. A proper noun is the name of a particular person, place, or thing.

Ms. Garcia is going to New Orleans on Tuesday.

Reflexive Pronoun. A reflexive pronoun, a personal pronoun to which -self or -selves has been added, refers to the subject and repeats its meaning.

We must discover the facts by ourselves.

Relative Pronoun. A relative pronoun introduces a dependent adjective clause and shows the relationship of the clause to the rest of the sentence.

He is one (<u>who</u> will succeed).

Restrictive Clause. A restrictive clause is a clause necessary to the meaning of the sentence.

The woman <u>who nodded</u> is our tennis champion.

Run-on Sentence. A run-on sentence, a definite error in punctuation, is composed of independent clauses not separated by any mark of punctuation.

I saw twenty large dolphin they leaped high into the air.

Sentence. A sentence is a group of words that express a complete thought.

Peace and prosperity are important to everyone.

Sentence Fragment. A sentence fragment is a group of words from which the subject, the predicate, or both have been omitted.

Seen across the barren wasteland.

Simple Sentence. A simple sentence has only one subject and one predicate, either of which may be compound.

Our <u>country</u> <u>has</u> a two-party political system.

Simple Subject. The simple subject is usually a noun or a pronoun that names the person, place, or thing about which something is said.

Many <u>people</u> were lost in the flood.

Subordinate Conjunction. A subordinate conjunction connects clauses of unequal value.

I came (<u>before</u> the whistle blew).

Suffix. A suffix is a letter or a syllable added to the end of a word to change the word's meaning.

If you agree, then we are all in agreement.

Synonyms. Synonyms are words with the same or similar meanings.

We will study the suggested <u>compromise</u>, but such a <u>settlement</u> may not be acceptable.

Tense. Tense denotes the time of action indicated by a verb.

The day <u>was</u> dark and dreary.

Verb. A verb is a word that shows action or a state of being.

This <u>is</u> my friend who <u>works</u> with me.

Verb Phrase. A verb phrase is a verb that is composed of two or more words.

We <u>should have given</u> the signal earlier.

Verbs of Condition. The verbs of condition (*seem, sound, appear, grow, look, prove, become, stand, feel, smell, turn,* and *taste*) are usually classed as action verbs but may be used as being verbs when no action is expressed.

I <u>feel</u> good today, but you <u>appear</u> ill.

Capitalization

Capitalize:

1. The first word of every sentence
2. The first word of every line of poetry
3. Titles when used before proper names
4. The names of particular persons, places, or things
5. The names of cities, states, nations, and so on
6. The names of the days of the week, the months, and holidays
7. The names of religious sects, ethnic or racial groups, and political parties
8. All names referring to the Deity, including personal pronouns, and to the Bible
9. Special documents, business firms, historical events, geographic areas, and brand names
10. *North, east, west,* and *south* when they refer to a section of the country, but not when they represent directions
11. Titles of books, songs, pamphlets, and articles
12. Initials and abbreviations of proper nouns
13. Words denoting family relationship when the word takes the place of a proper name
14. The first word of the closing phrase of a business or friendly letter
15. The first word and all nouns in the salutation of a letter
16. The names of streets, roads, avenues, and so on

Punctuation

Use a period:

1. After a declarative sentence
2. After an imperative sentence
3. After initials and abbreviations

Use a comma (or commas):

1. Before a coordinating conjunction in a compound sentence
2. After an introductory adverb clause
3. To set off clauses that are nonrestrictive, or are not necessary to the meaning of the sentence
4. After conjunctive adverbs used to join the independent clauses of a compound sentence
5. To set off words of direct address
6. To set off a nonrestrictive appositive
7. To set off an expression that interrupts a sentence
8. To set off independent words and parenthetical expressions
9. To set off contradictory or contrasting words or phrases
10. To set off a long introductory prepositional phrase
11. To separate words, phrases, or clauses in a series
12. After the salutation of a friendly letter
13. After the closing of all letters
14. To set off a direct quotation from the name of the speaker

Use a question mark after an interrogative sentence.

Use a semicolon:

1. Between the clauses of a compound sentence when a conjunction is not used
2. Between the clauses of a compound sentence that contains a conjunction if one or both of the clauses contain commas

3. Before conjunctive adverbs that join independent clauses

Use a colon:

1. To introduce a list of items given after the words *the following, as follows,* and *these words*
2. In a business letter after the salutation

3. To introduce a long or formal quotation

Use an exclamation point:

1. After an exclamatory sentence

2. After an interjection

Use quotation marks:

1. To enclose the exact words of the speaker
2. To enclose the names of short literary works, such as poems and magazine articles

3. To enclose nicknames or slang expressions

Use an apostrophe:

1. To form the possessive of nouns
2. To form the possessive of singular indefinite pronouns

3. To indicate the omission of letters in contractions

Use a dash:

1. To indicate a break in thought within the sentence

2. To set off an appositive or a parenthetical expression that has internal punctuation

Use a hyphen:

1. In compound numbers from twenty-one through ninety-nine
2. In many compound nouns and adjectives
3. To divide syllables at the end of a line of writing

Forming Plurals

To form the plural of nouns:

1. Add -*s* to nouns that *s* can unite without forming a separate syllable.
2. Add -*es* to nouns ending in -*sh, -ch, -s, -x,* or -*z.*
3. Add -*es* to nouns ending in -*y* when *y* is preceded by a consonant.
4. Change the final *y* to *i* and add -*es* when *y* is preceded by a consonant.
5. Add -*s* to nouns ending in -*o* when *o* is preceded by a vowel.
6. Add -*es* to nouns ending in -*o* when *o* is preceded by a consonant.
7. Add -*s* to almost all nouns ending in -*f* or -*fe*. Memorize nouns in which *f* or *fe* is changed to *v* and -*es* is added.

knife	shelf	thief	leaf	loaf
life	self	half	sheaf	beef
wife	elf	calf	wolf	

8. Add only an -*s* to form the plural of musical terms that end in -*o.*
9. Add -*s* to the principal part of a compound noun.
10. Add an apostrophe and -*s* to form the plural of letters, figures, signs, and single words.

Parts of Speech

Noun

1. A noun is the name of a person, a place, or a thing.
2. The subject of a sentence is a noun or a pronoun.
3. A noun is a predicate nominative (predicate noun) when it completes a being verb and renames the subject.
4. A noun is used as a direct object when it receives the action of an action verb.
5. A noun is used as an indirect object when it shows for whom or to whom something is done.

Pronouns

A pronoun is a word that takes the place of a noun.

1. **Personal Pronoun**
   a. A personal pronoun may denote the person speaking, the person spoken to, or the person spoken of.
   b. The personal pronoun must have an antecedent.
   c. The personal pronouns *I, he, she, we,* and *they* are always used as a subject, a predicate nominative, or an appositive of a subject or predicate nominative.
   d. A pronoun that completes a being verb and renames the subject is a predicate nominative.
   e. A pronoun predicate nominative is interchangeable with the subject.
   f. The personal pronouns *me, him, her, us,* and *them* are used as direct objects, indirect objects, objects of prepositions, and appositives of objects.
   g. A personal pronoun used as a direct object will receive the action of an action verb.
   h. A personal pronoun that shows *to whom* or *for whom* something is done is used as an indirect object.
   i. A personal pronoun that completes the prepositional phrase is used as the object of a preposition.
   j. An apostrophe and *-s* are never used with personal pronouns to show possession.
   k. Possessive personal pronouns may become adjectives if they are used as modifiers.
   l. Compound personal pronouns are formed by adding *-self* or *-selves* to some of the personal pronouns.
   m. When a pronoun introduces a gerund, the pronoun is usually in the possessive case.

2. **Relative Pronoun:**
   a. A relative pronoun may introduce an adjective clause.
   b. The relative pronoun will show the relationship of the dependent clause and the independent clause.
   c. The relative pronouns that introduce adjective clauses are *who, whom, which, whose,* and *that.* Sometimes *where* is used as a relative pronoun.
   d. Relative pronouns may introduce noun clauses.
   e. The relative pronoun *what* may also introduce a noun clause.
   f. The relative pronoun *who* is used as a subject.
   g. The relative pronoun *whom* is used as an object.

3. **Demonstrative Pronoun:**
   a. A demonstrative pronoun *points out.*
   b. The demonstrative pronouns are *this, that, these,* and *those.*

4. **Interrogative Pronoun:**
   a. An interrogative pronoun introduces a question.
   b. The interrogative pronouns are *who, whom, whose, which,* and *what.*

5. **Indefinite Pronoun:**
   a. An indefinite pronoun does not refer to a definite antecedent.
   b. Almost all indefinite pronouns are singular in number and require a singular verb.
   c. The plural indefinite pronouns are *both, many, several,* and *few.*

d. The indefinite pronouns *none, all* and *some* may be either singular or plural.

e. The singular indefinite pronouns form the possessive by adding an apostrophe and *-s*.

f. If no gender is indicated, the masculine gender or both the masculine and feminine genders are used with indefinite pronouns.

6. Intensive and Reflexive Pronouns:

a. The intensive and the reflexive pronouns are personal pronouns to which *-self* or *-selves* has been added.

b. The intensive pronoun emphasizes by repetition.

c. The reflexive pronoun turns back the action of the subject.

d. The reflexive pronoun will be the object of a verb or a preposition.

e. A reflexive pronoun is never used unless it has an antecedent subject.

f. The intensive and reflexive pronouns are never a part of a simple or a compound subject.

g. Do not use the expression *hisself* and *theirselves*.

h. Use the indefinite *one* with *oneself*.

Verbs

1. Being Verb:

a. Being verbs are sometimes called linking verbs.

b. The being verbs are: *is, are, am, was, were,* and all other forms of the verb *be*.

c. Being verbs of condition are: *seem, appear, look, feel, sound, turn, become, prove, stand, grow, smell,* and *taste*.

d. The "condition verbs" may also be action verbs when an action is indicated.

e. Being verbs are completed by subject complements, predicate nouns, or predicate adjectives.

f. Being verbs become helping verbs when used in a verb phrase to show tense.

g. Being verbs, as well as action verbs, must agree with the subject in number.

2. Action Verb:

a. Action verbs are divided into two classes, regular and irregular.

b. Regular verbs form the past tense and the past participle tense by adding *-d, -ed,* or *-t* to the present tense.

c. Regular verbs may end in a single consonant preceded by a vowel. This final consonant must be doubled before *-ed* is added.

d. A few regular verbs end in *-y*. If *y* is preceded by a consonant, the *y* is changed to *i* before *-ed* is added.

e. Some irregular verbs form the past and the past participle by changing the vowel within the verb.

f. Other irregular verbs form the past and the past participle by completely changing the word.

g. In some instances, the present, the past, and the past participle of an irregular verb are the same.

h. A singular action verb must be used with a singular subject.

i. A plural action verb must be used with a plural subject.

j. A phrase between the subject and the verb does not change the number of the verb.

Modifiers

1. Adjective:

a. An adjective is a word that modifies a noun or a pronoun.

b. An adjective modifies by describing, limiting, or pointing out.

c. Adjectives tell *which one, what kind,* or *how many.*

d. A descriptive adjective tells what kind of person, place, or thing the noun is.

e. A limiting adjective tells *which one* or *how many.*

f. A predicate adjective completes a being verb and describes the subject.

g. *The, an,* and *a* are adjectives that are called *articles.*

2. Adverb:

a. An adverb modifies a verb, an adjective, or another adverb.

b. Adverbs tell *how, when, where, why,* and *how much.*

c. Adverbs modify a verb or a verb phrase.

d. The simple adverb will express manner, place, time, degree, or number.

e. An interrogative adverb introduces a question.

f. The interrogative adverbs are *where, when, why,* and *how.*

g. A negative adverb denies or contradicts.

h. Two negative adverbs should not be used together in a sentence.

Connectives

1. Preposition:

a. A preposition connects its object (noun or pronoun) with some other word in the sentence.

b. A preposition is the first word in a prepositional phrase.

c. The object of the preposition is the noun or the pronoun that follows the preposition.

d. A prepositional phrase is never a basic part of a sentence.

e. A prepositional phrase will not include any of the basic elements of the sentence, such as the subject, the predicate, or the direct object, and so on.

2. Conjunction:

a. A conjunction connects words, phrases, and clauses.

b. A coordinate conjunction connects words or clauses of equal rank.

c. Correlative conjunctions are coordinate conjunctions used in pairs.

d. Subordinate conjunctions are used to join clauses of unequal value. Subordinate conjunctions are used in complex sentences.

e. Conjunctive adverbs are connectives used to join independent clauses.

PRETEST

Page 5. 1. 2, 3; **2.** 1, 3; **3.** 2, 3; **4.** 1, 4; **5.** 2, 3; **6.** 1, 4; **7.** 1, 3; **8.** 2, 3; **9.** 1, 3;

Page 6. 10. 1, 4; **11.** 2, 3; **12.** 2, 3; **13.** 1, 3; **14.** 2; **15.** 2, 4; **16.** 2, 3; **17.** 1, 4; **18.** 1, 3; **19.** 1, 3; **20.** 1, 4; **21.** 1, 3; **22.** 2, 4; **23.** 2, 4; **24.** 1, 4; **25.** 2, 4;

Page 7. 26. 2, 3; **27.** 2, 4; **28.** 1, 2; **29.** 1, 3; **30.** 1, 4; **31.** 2, 4; **32.** 2, 3; **33.** 1, 4; **34.** 2, 3; **35.** 1, 4.

UNIT 1: Using Sentences

LESSON I: The Sentence

Page 8. Practice 1. Fragments changed into sentences will vary. 1. F; 2. S, Have you met Mr. Moore? 3. S, Please give me the tack hammer.

Page 9. 4. F; 5. F; 6. S, The personnel manager gave me an application blank to fill out. 7. S, Good mechanics are usually well paid for their work. 8. S, Where is my new shirt? 9. S, Hey, Bill, I got a raise today! 10. F; 11. S, Empty the ice bag here. 12. S, That was an interesting story about Joe Lopez in Sunday's paper. 13. S, When will you be ready to take the driving test? 14. F; 15. S, Fifty dollars is a ridiculous price for that dress. 16. S, How long have you been working at the machine shop? 17. S, I bought a good-looking shirt at the half-price sale. 18. S, Let's take the kids on a picnic next Saturday. 19. F.

Page 10. Practice 2. 2. The efficiency of a machine is always less than 100 percent. Perhaps you can explain why. 3. Who made the first wheel? We do not know. The first wheels were probably square. Time brought about changes and improvements. 4. Did you hear the news? We will have to wait an hour for the doctor. 5. A ship loaded with cargo was anchored in the harbor. Suddenly we heard a loud explosion. Almost immediately smoke began to rise from the stern. 6. What a wonderful magician she is! Have you seen her act? She has been on television. 7. We caught the bus at 8:15. It always seems to be late. 8. Don't be upset. I'll help you paint the room in the morning. 9. I went to the market and purchased some fish. Then I took them home and cooked them. 10. Take the package to the office and give it to Mrs. Stanton. Then come back here quickly. 11. Always shop here. You can buy things at a lower price.

Page 11. Practice 3. Sentences will vary.

LESSON II: Two Kinds of Sentences

Page 12. Practice 1. The rain had stopped, and we could see a rainbow in the distance. 2. We must call the ranger at once, or he won't be able to photograph the bear. 3. She passed the test easily, but many more tests lay ahead. 4. De Soto searched for gold; however, he found the villages of the Pueblo people.

Page 13. 5. The boy would listen to no one, nor would he think for himself. 6. The native performers sang songs of joy; consequently, the hours seemed shorter. 7. The man grumbled, and then he walked away. 8. Mice have been used for experiments, and many people don't like the idea. **Practice 2.** Sentences and punctuation will vary. Be sure that a semicolon comes before and a comma follows each conjunctive adverb. **Practice 3.** Conjunctive adverbs will vary. A semicolon should come before and a comma follow each conjunctive adverb.

Page 14. Practice 4. 1. c, 2. c, 3. d, 4. a, 5. c.

LESSON III: Complex Sentences

Page 15. Practice 1. The following subordinate conjunctions should be underlined: 1. When, 2. wherever, 3. if, 4. While, 5. until, 6. until.

Page 16. Practice 2. 1. When Tseng reached for the wrench, he tripped. 2. (You) Put this bouquet of yellow roses where everyone can see it. 3. The plants that grew in this garden came from Japan. 4. Although you may not believe it, we are really working hard for you. 5. Did you tell Ernesto that I want to see him this morning? 6. Before you go to work, (you) please sweep the front porch and the steps. 7. Jane O'Leary, who is visiting us, sells new cars in Chicago.

Page 17. 8. The city has doubled in size since you moved away ten years ago. 9. Aunt Rebecca, who is a minister, told us that you **were coming** here soon. 10. The **person** who saved the drowning boy **was awarded** a **medal**. 11. As I passed the crowd in the park, **I noticed** many small children. 12. **(You) Do not leave** until the car is repaired. 13. **Mr. Jenkins**, who works at our plant, **won** a prize in the contest. 14. **All are to stand** while the flag **is being raised**. 15. The **accident**, which could have been prevented easily, **caused** much damage. 16. Since the utility **bill is** due today, **I will pay** it at the utility office. **Practice 3.** Sentences will vary.

UNIT REVIEW

Page 18. 1. 4, **2.** 2, **3.** 1, **4.** 3, **5.** 2, **6.** 3, **7.** 1,
Page 19. 8. 4, **9.** 1, **10.** 2, **11.** 1, **12.** Sentences will vary. **13.** Sentences will vary. **14.** Sentences will vary.

UNIT 2: Verbs

LESSON I: Being Verbs

Page 20. Practice. 1. You, appear; 2. I, have been; 3. I, am, I, am; 4. work, seems, it, is; 5. hotels, were; 6. Has, supervisor, been.

LESSON II: Action Verbs and Verb Phrases

Page 21. Practice 1. 1. I, knocked; 2. politician, made, who, listened; 3. referee, gave; 4. they, announced, we, went; 5. supervisor, posted; 6. shelter, we, found, gave; 7. he, received; 8. we, reached, Jeanne, ran, 9. You, must climb, look; 10. Steve, laughed, spoiled; 11. Lightning, struck, flames, rose; 12. volunteers, assist; 13. we, wore. **Practice 2.** 1. said—A, will be—B; 2. should be—B; 3. cook—A, must be—B, are—B; 4. is—B, would buy—A; 5. is—B, will throw—A, 6. is—B, got—A, wanted—A.

Page 22. Practice 3. These verbs should be underlined twice: 1. heard, say, may leave; 2. are known, is; 3. returned, were checked; 4. is, remains; 5. has been done, will accept; 6. has been found; 7. can expect, sit; 8. were seeing, were; 9. was, lost; 10. Were told; 11. were ordered, sent; 12. will be, live; 13. can find, get; 14. could hear, communicated; 15. calls, return, will call.

LESSON III: Verb Tense

Page 24. Practice 1. helped, helped; 2. plan, planned; 3. marched, marched; 4. hurry, hurried; 5. startled, startled;

Page 25. 6. comply, complied; 7. omit, omitted; 8. shopped, shopped; 9. tick, ticked; 10. barred, barred; 11. played, played; 12. smelled, smelled; 13. scurry, scurried; 14. jarred, jarred; 15. tapped, tapped; 16. ask, asked; 17. desire, desired; 18. reply, replied; 19. rallied, rallied; 20. notice, noticed; 21. propped, propped; 22. tape, taped; 23. shipped, shipped; 24. handle, handled; 25. move, moved; 26. carry, carried; 27. bragged, bragged; 28. check, checked; 29. trapped, trapped; 30. dived, dived; 31. stared, stared; 32. married, married.

Page 28. Practice 2. Sentences will vary. **Practice 3.** 1. hidden; 2. mistaken; 3. sunk; 4. stolen; 5. hid; 6. saw; 7. thrown; 8. rang; 9. done; 10. sprung; 11. threw; 12. burst.

Page 29. Practice 4. 1. Let; 2. set; 3. can; 4. lay; 5. drunk; 6. gone; 7. taught; 8. lie; 9. swum; 10. sat; 11. eaten; 12. written; 13. choose.

LESSON IV: Subject and Verb Agreement

Page 30. Practice 1. 1. is; 2. were; 3. doesn't; 4. are; 5. are; 6. Were; 7. Don't; 8. are.

Page 31. Practice 2. 1. has; 2. was; 3. looks; 4. need; 5. stands.

LESSON V: Contractions

Page 32. Practice 1. 1. doesn't; 2. Isn't; 3. hasn't; 4. weren't; 5. Who's; 6. it's; 7. There's; 8. you're; 9. aren't;

Page 33. 10. whose; 11. haven't; 12. it's; 13. It's, its; 14. they're, their. **Practice 2.** 1. It's, its; 2. You're, your; 3. Their, their; 4. Who's; 5. Your, your; 6. There's, theirs; 7. Its, it's; 8. Your, your; 9. your; 10. you're, your. **Practice 3.** These verbs should be underlined twice: 1. will be surprised, tell; 2. might have been injured, had moved; 3. grew, rolled; 4. struggled; 5. sat, opened, yawned; 6. came, was; 7. had sung, had; 8. Do forget, arrive; 9. had drunk; 10. needed, searched; 11. have seen, do remember; 12. had built, would have gone; 13. was, knew; 14. has blown, has blown; 15. are; 16. is, require; 17. were, was, were; 18. Did, leave, became; 19. have grown, have become.

UNIT REVIEW

Page 34. 1. 2, 4; **2.** 1, 3; **3.** 1, 3; **4.** 2, 4; **5.** 2, 3; **6.** 1, 4; **7.** 1, 3; **8.** 1, 3; **9.** 1, 4; **10.** 2, 3; **11.** 2, 3; **12.** 2, 4; **13.** 1, 4.

UNIT 3: Nouns

LESSON I: Common, Proper, and Collective Nouns

Page 35. Practice 1. These nouns should be underlined: 1. Santos Garza[P], application, Low's Department Store[C]; 2. statement, First National Bank[C], deposit, May[P]; 3. Joan[P], brochure[C], tour[C], France[P], Switzerland[P]; 4. Wheat[C], Kansas[P], number[C], states[C], Middle West[P]; 5. Dr. Vincent[P], friend[C], hospital[C], pains[C]; 6. Disneyland[P], trip[C], California[P]; 7. Brown Building[P], Market Street[P], Main Street[P]; 8. manager[C], store[C], complaints[C], office[C], Miami[P].

Page 36. Practice 2. 1. family, is going—S; 2. jury, were—P; 3. class, were—P; 4. group, shouts—S; 5. company, is raising—S; 6. committee, was meeting—S; 7. choir, is singing—S; 8. audience, was, responded—S; 9. team, plans—S; 10. flock, flies—S; 11. group, takes—S; 12. army, marches—S.

LESSON II: Plural Nouns

Page 38. Practice 1. 1. halves, 2. geese, 3. knives, 4. sheep, 5. boys, 6. pianos, 7. chairs, 8. ladies, 9. tomatoes, 10. passes, 11. boxes, 12. oxen, 13. men, 14. tears, 15. children.
Practice 2. jungles, countries, animals, trees, hundreds, monkeys, lives, animals, kangaroos, deer, moose, limbs, waters, pools, fish, trout, piles, bushes, fishers.

Page 39. flocks, geese, birds, monkeys, lions, tigers, panthers, voices, seconds, shelters, havens, beasts. **Practice 3.** Detroit[S], the largest city[S] in Michigan[S] and known as the automobile capital[S] of the nation[S], is an interesting city[S] to visit. Besides gleaming show windows[P] that display the latest automobiles[P], there are many attractions[P] that appeal to visitors[P]. The Detroit Zoological Park[S] contains wild animals[P] that live in outdoor settings[P] without bars[P] or cages[P]. In Greenfield Village[S]— located in Dearborn[S], a suburb[S] of Detroit[S]—are many historic buildings[P] brought to the area[S] and restored by Henry Ford[S]. Crafts[P] by American artists[P] and a fine display[S] of old and new automobiles[P] are exhibited nearby in the Henry Ford Museum[S]. Detroit[S] has many parks[P] for recreation[S], including the beautiful Belle Isle[S], an island[S] in the Detroit River[S]. One popular attraction[S] is the Renaissance Center[S], with its four tall office buildings[S], a 73-story hotel[S], and shopping malls[P]. San Francisco[P], a fascinating port[S] in California[S], is the favorite city[S] of many Americans[P]. Perhaps the most colorful part[S] of the city[S] is Chinatown[S], a section[S] of San Francisco[S] that every visitor[S] should experience. Its narrow streets[S], Oriental architecture[P], and interesting shops[P] and restaurants[P] create an atmosphere[S] not found in any other American city[S]. A drive[S] across the Golden Gate Bridge[S], a fish dinner[S] at Fisherman's Wharf[S], a visit[S] to Nob Hill[S] a dinner[S] at a Chinese restaurant[S], and a ride[S] on a cable car[S] are a few[P] of the experiences[P] that visitors[P] will long remember. There are also many fine parks[P] and museums[P] in the city[S]. Fans[P] of classical music[S] might attend a concert[S] or one of San Francisco's[S] famous opera productions[P]. (San Francisco's[P] in the last sentence is a possessive noun. These nouns will be studied in the next lesson.)

LESSON III: Possessive Nouns

Page 40. Practice 1. 1. d,
Page 41. 2. c, 3. a, 4. a, 5. b, 6. b, 7. a, 8. c, 9. a. **Practice 2.** 1. man's hat, 2. Jane's husband, 3. Lucy's garden, 4. officer's report, 5. cat's claws, 6. employee's job, 7. country's army, 8. child's book.

LESSON IV: Uses of Nouns

Page 42. Practice 1. Underline these predicate nouns: 1. part; 2. president; 3. secretary; 4. person; 5. fracture; 6. branch; 7. wilderness; 8. Alaska, Texas, California. **Practice 2.** Underline these nouns used in direct address: 1. friends, 2. Ms. Gonzales, 3. Mary, 4. folks, 5. Ladies, gentlemen, Carlos Artega.

Page 43. Practice 3. 1. $\overset{DA}{\text{Ruth}}$, fair, $\overset{S}{}$ $\overset{PN}{\text{responsibility}}$; 2. Charles Atlas, $\overset{S}{\text{strongman}}$, $\overset{PN}{}$ $\overset{PN}{\text{expert}}$; 3. Elizabeth, queen, India, nation; 4. $\overset{S}{\text{Cupful}}$, $\overset{S}{\text{handful}}$, $\overset{S}{\text{spoonful}}$, $\overset{S}{\text{carload}}$, $\overset{PN}{\text{units}}$; 5. $\overset{DA}{\text{George}}$, $\overset{S}{\text{flowers}}$; 6. University of Iowa, $\overset{S}{\text{school}}$; 7. $\overset{S}{\text{Tea}}$, $\overset{PN}{\text{drink}}$; 8. Boating, fishing, $\overset{S}{\text{sports}}$; 9. president, $\overset{PN}{\text{commander-in-chief}}$; 10. $\overset{S}{\text{word}}$, $\overset{PN}{\text{verb}}$; 11. pedagogues, $\overset{S}{\text{slaves}}$; 12. Mathematics, $\overset{PN}{\text{subject}}$; 13. Chicago, $\overset{S}{\text{city}}$; 14. Tornadoes, $\overset{S}{\text{storms}}$; 15. $\overset{DA}{\text{Boris}}$; 16. Juan, $\overset{PN}{\text{owner}}$; 17. Doris, $\overset{S}{\text{person}}$, $\overset{DA}{\text{Don}}$; 18. White House, $\overset{S}{\text{home}}$; 19. Tomas, Phil, $\overset{S}{\text{trip}}$; 20. Marta, $\overset{PN}{\text{senator}}$; 21. flavors, vanilla, $\overset{PN}{\text{chocolate}}$, $\overset{PN}{\text{peach}}$; 22. Herb, $\overset{PN}{\text{mechanic}}$.

LESSON V: Nouns Used as Objects

Page 44. Practice 1. 1. Circle *Gay*; underline *car* and *test*; 2. Underline *memories*; 3. Underline *curb*; 4. Underline *permit*; 5. Underline *Declaration of Independence*; 6. Underline *millions*; 7. Circle *children*; underline *much*; 8. Underline *hundreds*; 9. Circle *Stan*; underline *instructions*; 10. Circle *Betty*; underline *story*;

Page 45. 11. Circle *us*; underline *health, wealth,* and *time;* 12. Underline *trip* and *mode;* 13. Underline *migration*; 14. Underline *friendliness* and *interest*; 15. Underline *tent, boxes,* and *keys*; circle *Mary*. **Practice 2.** Sentences will vary. **Practice 3.** Put parentheses around these prepositional phrases: 1. of people, on television, on the moon; 2. of the tide, across the sand, over the wall; 3. in the wheelchair, of this office; 4. about the United States, about the country's way of life;

Page 46. 5. Down the side, of the mountain, of nomads; 6. of literature, on the mood, of the reader; 7. at the plant, by the employees; 8. for herself, in the Air Force; 9. During the Revolutionary War, across the mountains. **Practice 4.** 1. The street, a broad thoroughfare, really is an avenue. 2. The house, a colonial mansion, stands on the summit of a high hill. 3. Germany, a country in Europe, was once overrun by the Huns, a warlike tribe. 4. The Liberty Bell, the most famous bell in our country, may be seen in Philadelphia. 5. If you plan to travel in Mexico, our neighbor to the south, you should purchase Mexican insurance. 6. Our state's *Vehicle Code,* a book of highway rules, is seldom read by motorists. 7. One of our magnificent sights is the Grand Canyon, a masterpiece of erosion. 8. Mark Twain, the author, lived near the Mississippi River. 9. Few people live in Alaska, a land

of many contrasts. **Practice 5.** 1. Animals—S, plains—OP, America—OP, people—S, land—DO; 2. father-in-law—S, business—OP, success—OP;

Page 47. 3. People—S, Dark Ages—OP, advantages—DO, comforts—DO; 4. Ms. Smith—S, secretary-treasurer—PN, club—OP, she—S, president—DO; 5. Mrs. Garcia—S, daughter—S, lecture—DO, discussion—A, art—OP; 6. money—S, country—OP, wampum—PN, beads—A, shells—OP; 7. pieces—S, eight—OP, Milton—DA, coins—PN, colonists'—P, pockets—OP; 8. ball—S, pitcher—OP, she—S, base—OP, out—OP; 9. son—S, reader—PN, Carl—DA, he—S, movements—.DO; 10. car—S, lifeguard—IO, resuscitator—DO, beach—OP. **Practice 6.** Sentences will vary.

UNIT REVIEW

Page 48. **1.** 4; **2.** 1, 2; **3.** 5; **4.** 3; **5.** 3; **6.** 5; **7.** 1; **8.** 4.

UNIT 4: Pronouns

LESSON I: Kinds of Pronouns

Page 49. Practice 1. 1. ⬭Carlos and Virginia⬭ will have to finish their work before they can leave. 2. Each ⬭woman⬭ showed $\overset{her}{\text{their}}$ pass before entering the building. 3. ⬭Mandy⬭ you must have your car inspected this month. 4. Each ⬭dog⬭ on that farm has had $\overset{its}{\text{their}}$ vaccinations. 5. That ⬭hospital⬭ has its own generator in case there is a power failure.

Page 50. Practice 2. 1. his, 2. her, 3. their, 4. its.

Page 51. Practice 3. 1. I; 2. us; 3. my; 4. she, them; 5. theirs, ours; 6. them; 7. We; 8. she, your; 9. us; 10. she; 11. he, 12. me.

Page 52. Practice 4. 1. I; 2. her; 3. him; 4. he; 5. me; 6. she; 7. She and I; 8. yours, he and I; 9. he; 10. her; 11. me; 12. him, her; 13. me.

Page 53. Practice 5. 1. his, 2. your, 3. his, 4. she, 5. their, 6. I. **Practice 6.** 1. c, 2. d, 3. d, 4. a, 5. c, 6. a, 7. b.

LESSON II: Relative Pronouns

Page 54. Practice 1. 1. that escaped last night, 2. whose name was drawn at the automobile show, 3. which shirt looks better with these slacks, 4. that I would not be coming to work today, 5. that is on the left, 6. that you are sorry about your actions, 7. that she would be late coming to work today, 8. whose work orders are posted.

Page 55. Practice 2. 1. who won the prize, 2. that tell about Africa, 3. that is useable.

Page 56. 4. whose employees will attend, 5. that were given to the family, 6. whom I have not met, 7. that is open, 8. that is repeated, 9. who will be able to do the work, 10. whom he was speaking, 11. who is now a citizen, 12. who is sitting at the first desk, 13. which was soft and comforting, 14. which now hangs in the mill, 15. that had been destroyed, 16. whose names were on the overtime list, 17. who did not accept his theory, 18. which rose above the city, 19. who wait and work, 20. whom you represent, 21. which sounded like the voices of angels, 22. that is needed for the first trip, 23. who are not through, 24. who is the builder of the boats, that sail this lake, 25. whom we were to deliver the package, 26. that I will be gone for several weeks, 27. whoever pays my price, 28. who delivers papers, 29. that I purchased, 30. whoever opens the door, 31. whom we saw.

LESSON III: Demonstrative and Interrogative Pronouns

Page 57. Practice 1. 1. This—D; 2. what—I;
Page 58. 3. That—D, this—D; 4. Who—I; 5. whom—I; 6. those—D; 7. those—D; 8. These—D, which—I; 9. Who—I; 10. What—I; these—D; 11. Whose—I, that—D; 12. that—D, this—D; 13. those—D; 14. Which—I; **Practice 2.** Sentences will vary.

LESSON IV: Indefinite Pronouns

Page 59. Practice 1. 1. is; 2. were; 3. his; 4. she; 5. his or her; 6. were; 7. is, she or he;
Page 60. 8. are; 9. is; 10. knows; 11. expects; 12. is; 13. have, their; 14. was; 15. was; 16. has, its; 17. were; 18. feels; 19. needs; 20. is, his or her; 21. have. **Practice 2.** Sentences will vary.

LESSON V: Intensive and Reflexive Pronouns

Page 61. Practice 1. 1. myself; 2. I; 3. themselves;

Page 62. 4. themselves; 5. themselves; 6. himself or herself; 7. yourselves; 8. themselves; 9. me; 10. we. **Practice 2.** 1. hers; 2. me; 3. whom; 4. We, him, himself; 5. those, her or his; 6. whom, her; 7. themselves; 8. me, himself; 9. its; 10. she, him; 11. who, them; 12. us, ourselves; 13. were, us; 14. is, me. **Practice 3.** 1. a, 2. b, 3. a, 4. d.

UNIT REVIEW

Page 63. 1. 1, 3; **2.** 1, 4; **3.** 2, 4; **4.** 2, 4; **5.** 1, 3.

Page 64. 6. 1, 3; **7.** 1, 4; **8.** 1, 3; **9.** 1, 4; **10.** 1, 4; **11.** 2, 3; **12.** 2, 3; **13.** 2, 3.

UNIT 5: Adjectives and Adverbs
LESSON I: Adjectives

Page 65. Practice. Underline these adjectives: 1. The, elderly, two, successful; 2. swift, sure, a, small; 3. the, diving, the, the, blue; 4. This, simple, expensive, useful; 5. The, red, blue, green, gold, the; 6. Many, the, tiny, lovely.

LESSON II: Adverbs

Page 66. Practice 1. Underline these adverbs: 1. constantly, never; 2. forward, carefully, not, too, quickly; 3. extremely, effectively; 4. almost; 5. now, later.
Page 67. 6. seldom, early, very, slowly; 7. Angrily, loudly; 8. well, extremely; 9. surely, ever; 10. Where, unusually; 11. quickly, soon; 12. recently, 13. no adverbs; 14. brightly; 15. confidently, firmly; 16. lazily, where; 17. quite, rapidly. **Practice 2.** Sentences will vary.

LESSON III: Comparison of Adjectives and Adverbs

Page 69. Practice 1. more, most; 2. stingier, stingiest; 3. less, least; 4. more rapid, most rapid; 5. redder, reddest; 6. better, best; 7. sweeter, sweetest; 8. worse; worst; 9. later, latest; 10. worse, worst; 11. more honest, most honest; 12. sooner, soonest; 13. happier, happiest; 14. faster, fastest; 15. more useful, most useful; 16. dustier, dustiest; 17. more cruelly, most cruelly; 18. earlier, earliest; 19. more quickly, most quickly; 20. newer, newest; 21. kinder, kindest; 22. (leave blank). **Practice 2.** 2. away—adv., fully—adv., that—adj., very—adv., difficult—adj.;

Page 70. 3. new—adj., more—adv., carefully—adv., nearly—adv., fatal—adj.; 4. that—adj., unusually—adv., exciting—adj., forever—adv., 5. much—adj., useful—adj., interesting—adj.; 6. Many—adj., all—adj., this—adj., the—adj., California—adj.; 7. The—adj., champion—adj., the—adj., second—adj., weak—adj.; 8. Those—adj., calm—adj., brave—adj., also—adv., unusually—adv., careless—adj.; 9. An—adj., ideal—adj., a—adj., simple—adj., a—adj., beautiful—adj.; 10. constantly—adv., many—adj., bad—adj.; 11. Why—adv., n't—adv., very—adv., late—adj.; 12. There—adv., scarcely—adv., any—adj., the—adj., many—adj., the—adj.; 13. much—adv., too—adv., dark—adj., the—adj., beautiful—adj.; 14. down—adv., early—adv., the—adj., over—adv., five—adj.; 15. The—adj., steadily—adv., worse—adj., the—adj.; 16. constantly—adv., that—adj., new—adj.; 17. The—adj., the—adj., two—adj., carefully—adv., then—adv., reluctantly—adv.; 18. certainly—adv., readily—adv., unfortunate—adj.; 19. now—adv., then—adv., always—adv., very—adv., glad—adj.; 20. last—adj., amazingly—adv., clever—adj., extremely—adv., valuable—adj.; 21. this—adj., bus—adj., definitely—adv., too—adv., old—adj., any—adj.; 22. The—adj., extensive—adj., the—adj., almost—adv., completely—adv.; 23. recently—adv., great—adj.; 24. repeatedly—adv., poor—adj., usually—adv., beautifully—adv.; 25. The—adj., most—adv., difficult—adj., today—adv.; 26. accurately—adv., the—adj., the—adj., too—adv., obscured—adj., the—adj., poor—adj.; 27. The—adj., many—adj., each—adj.; 28. The—adj., particularly—adv., refreshing—adj., long—adj.; 29. This—adj., extremely—adv., cold—adj., many—adj., fruit—adj.

UNIT REVIEW

Page 71. 1. 2; 2. 5; 3. 3; 4. 4; 5. 1.

UNIT 6: Prepositions, Conjunctions, and Interjections

LESSON: How Prepositions, Conjunctions, and Interjections Are Used

Page 72. Practice 1. Underline these prepositional phrases: 1. toward the south, after dawn; 2. of twelve people, by the judge; 3. by the applause, from the crowd, of spectators; 4. at the far end, of the mall; 5. Because of the storms, to the concert.

Page 73. 6. In the afternoon, in the hospital, for several hours; 7. Beyond the hills, in a blaze, of color; 8. at dawn, in the tower; 9. of us, except Ralph, along the river, for several hours. **Practice 2.** 1. Since—sub., neither—cor., nor—cor.; 2. where—sub., and—coor.; 3. and—coor.; 4. Either—cor., or—cor.; 5. because—sub.; 6. Unless—sub., and—coor.

Page 74. Practice 3. Conjunctions will vary. Suggested: 1. Both, and; 2. but; 3. When, and; 4. Both, and; 5. and; 6. Neither, nor; 7. Since; 8. When, and; 9. or; 10. and, and; 11. until; 12. and, before; 13. Since; 14. but; 15. lest; 16. Either, or; 17. Since.

UNIT REVIEW

Page 75. 1. 4; 2. 2; 3. 2; 4. 5; 5. 2, 3; 6. 4; 7. 1, 2; 8. 5.

UNIT 7: Punctuation
LESSON I: Punctuation Marks

Page 76. Practice 1. 1. Sarah Jane is asking someone to leave. 2. Jane is asking Sarah to leave. 3. John Victor will do the signing.

Page 77. 4. John is being told that Victor will sign the time card. 5. The employee found a new job. 6. The contractor found a new job. **Practice 2.** 1. Didn't they move to the U.S.A. recently? 2. Mr. and Mrs. Garza paid 99 cents for a lb. of grapes. 3. Watch out for that snake! 4. Who can tell us some interesting sights to visit in Washington, D.C. next week? 5. This shirt is $14.95, but that shirt is only $12.95. 6. Can't you tell me how to fix a flat? 7. Run for your lives! 8. Dr. Barraza, didn't you tell me to take this medicine once a day? 9. That job was too easy, and Mrs. Goodman did not enjoy it. 10. Please tell Dr. and Mrs. McNutt that I can sell them 20 lbs. of shelled pecans. 11. Mr. and Mrs. Rudy Gonzales own that department store. 12. This U.S. postage stamp is very old. 13. When will we be able to buy a lb. of grass seeds?

LESSON II: Using Commas

Page 78. Practice 1. Conjunctions added will vary.

Page 79. Practice 2. 1. You may go if you wish, though I think it is a mistake. 2. My cousin, who is a good tennis player, will arrive today. 3. If you are determined to succeed, you will work hard for success. 4. I have worked all day, Elaine; nevertheless, there is much to be done. 5. George should not be so unhappy, for the hard times should not last long. 6. Harry must make a decision soon, or it will be too late. 7. Allison, who is never on time, did not receive a raise this year. 8. When fall comes again, the birds will fly south. 9. The old bell, which once was rung on special occasions, is still there. 10. Grandmother's furniture was old and worn, but it was valuable to her. 11. Sandra was given a promotion; however, it will not be reported in this newsletter. 12. We cannot accept his resignation, as he alone knows the needed specifications. 13. Because many tourist attractions are offered, our chief industry is tourism. 14. No comma needed. 15. He blew the boat's whistle loudly, but the bridge did not rise. 16. No comma needed. 17. Since you left, I have been very lonesome. 18. No comma needed.

Page 80. Practice 3. 1. a, 2. d, 3. d,

Page 81. 4. b, 5. a, 6. c. **Practice 4.** 1. My brother's wife was born in London, England, twenty-nine years ago. 2. I filled out a sample form, checked the figures, and then copied it on the final form. 3. Dogs, cats, and chickens wandered aimlessly down the street. 4. That package must be declined by no later than Monday, May 3. 5. My aunt lives at 1821 Druid Drive, Memphis, Tennessee. 6. The truck ran off the road, jumped a ditch, and hit a tree. 7. On March 9, 1789, the Constitution became the law of the United States. 8. Bells rang, whistles blew, and people cried with joy and happiness. 9. From the burning forest fled deer, rabbits, bears, snakes, and other creatures. 10. The sun was low, red, and glowing when we reached the hilltop.

LESSON III: Using Semicolons, Colons, Dashes, and Apostrophes

Page 82. Practice 1. Semicolons should follow these words: 1. early; 2. shift; 3. o'clock; 4. still; 5. nervous.

Page 83. Practice 2. 1. The bus goes down these streets: Elm, Pine, and Maple. 2. The candidates—Smith, Garza, and Washington—will have a debate tonight. 3. Who made this statement: "Give me liberty or give me death!" 4. The pioneers—please pay attention, folks—suffered many hardships. 5. Tools, oil, water, and gloves—these are the things that must be packed. **Practice 3.** 1. I'm afraid you've failed to pay the insurance premium on time. 2. Don't you like the new color they've chosen to paint their house? 3. Sandra doesn't know if she's to work today. 4. Haven't you told them that this isn't a job they'll like? **Practice 4.** 1. They've weighed the evidence on both sides; it seems to balance. 2. Home, family, security, and health—these people seek. 3. If we're late, please say that we're coming.

Page 84. 4. There aren't any veterans of the Civil War now living. 5. This plan, and it's really

my own, will revolutionize industry. 6. You must be responsible for these items: blankets, pillows, sheets, and towels.

LESSON IV: Using Quotation Marks

Page 84. Practice 1. 1. Roberto asked, "Isn't it time to start counting the ballots?" 2. The boy replied, "No madam, we do not live here now." 3. "Get out of my boat!" Bill shouted as he ran toward the water. 4. Maria spoke quietly and said, "I saw the car when it passed." 5. "The water is deep," said Jerry, "and very cold." 6. Henry called to his father, "The car is washed and ready!" 7. "Yea, team! Rah! Rah!" shouted the crowd. 8. "You need to read your job description more carefully," said Morris.

Page 85. 9. "Long ago people ate with their fingers," she said. "There were no forks." 10. "No, I am not going," he said. "I do not have a car." 11. The librarian said to the boys, "Be quiet, please." 12. John and I thought that he said, "I will be there." 13. "Bring the water quickly!" the man shouted. **Practice 2.** Sentences may vary. Suggested: 1. The mayor said, "This project is essential to the future growth of the city." 2. Jane said to me, "I plan to resign at the end of this month." 3. I said, "We must finish this job before dark." 4. The doctor said, "You need this prescription." 5. The pharmacist said, "You shouldn't drive while taking this medicine."

Page 86. 6. The police officer said, "You were driving too fast." 7. You said, "Don is to arrive at the airport this afternoon." 8. Sandy said, "I will help you paint your bedroom." 9. I said, "I will be unable to work on your car this week." 10. "You will need to fill out an application blank," the personnel manager said. 11. Pat said, "A bridge is washed out on Highway 12." 12. I screamed, "A snake is under the car!" **Practice 3.** 1. Did you say that "The Raven" is your favorite poem? 2. "How To Find a Job" was the article in the magazine I enjoyed most. 3. "Teddy" is the nickname my parents gave me. 4. The "Star Spangled Banner" was written in the early 1800s. 5. My real name is James, but everyone calls me "Jimmy." 6. "The Night the Bed Fell" is a very funny story.

UNIT REVIEW

PAGE 87. 1. 2; 2. 3, 4; 3. 4; 4. 1, 2; 5. 5; 6. 1, 3; 7. 2; 8. 4; 9. 1, 2.

UNIT 8: Capitalization

LESSON: Using Capitalization

Page 89. Practice 1. The following words should be capitalized: 1. Iroquois Confederacy,

Indian, United States Constitution; 2. Athens, Sparta, Greece; 3. Ireland, Irish; 4. *Cannery Row*, John Steinbeck; 5. Everest Adult High School, Daytona, Florida; 6. Jewish, Catholic, Baptist, Buddhist; 7. Catholic, South America, American Southwest; 8. World War, Germany, France; 9. International Peace Gardens, United States, Canada; 10. July, Declaration of Independence, American; 11. Maple Road, Reno, Nevada, James; 12. Mother, Father; 13. *Torah*; 14. New York, France; 15. Prime Minister Churchill, Washington; 16. Democratic; 17. April, May, Southern California.

Page 90. Practice 2. 1. a, 2. a, 3. c,

Page 91. 4. b, 5. d, 6. c, 7. b, 8. c, 9. d, 10. a, 11. d.

UNIT REVIEW

Page 92. 1. 1; **2.** 1; **3.** 1, 2, 4; **4.** 1, 3, 4; **5.** 3, 4; **6.** 3, 4; **7.** 3, 4; **8.** 5;

Page 93. 9. 3; **10.** 3; **11.** 1, 3; **12.** 1, 3, 4; **13.** 2, 3, 4; **14.** 2, 3; **15.** 1, 4.

UNIT 9: Introduction to Correct Usage

LESSON I

Page 95. Practice 1. 1. aggravated; 2. all right; 3. effect; 4. between; 5. an, among; 6. already; 7. all together; 8. between; 9. isn't; 10. accept; 11. an; 12. all ready; 13. all right; 14. altogether; 15. between; 16. Accept.

Page 96. Practice 2. 1. d, 2. b, 3. m, 4. n, 5. c, 6. p, 7. e, 8. k, 9. g, 10. q, 11. i, 12. j, 13. a, 14. h, 15. l, 16. f, 17. o, 18. r.

LESSON II

Page 98. Practice. 1. bad; 2. as; 3. at, to; 4. group, anywhere; 5. Bring; 6. very; 7. beside, irritated; 8. everywhere; 9. as if; 10. as; 11. somewhere; 12. anywhere; 13. exceedingly; 14. beside; 15. so; 16. as; 17. Take; 18. as if; 19. bad; 20. group; 21. badly; 22. group; 23. as; 24. as if.

LESSON III

Page 100. Practice. 1. have; 2. calculate, can; 3. may, from; 4. enthusiastic; 5. burst; 6. think, etc.; 7. complexioned; 8. May; 9. burst; 10. think; 11. complexioned; 12. have; 13. charming; 14. from; 15. suppose; 16. enthusiastic; 17. have; 18. etc.,; 19. burst; 20. can; 21. suppose; 22. have; 23. from; 24. have; 25. from; 26. May; 27. can; 28. have.

LESSON IV

Page 102. Practice. 1. strange, farther; 2. into, in; 3. Teach; 4. Let; 5. from; 6. fewer; 7. farther; 8. in, into; 9. its; 10. from; 11. well, well; 12. into; 13. behind; 14. teach; 15. It's, it's; 16. into; 17. in, into; 18. behind; 19. good, well; 20. strange; 21. further, farther; 22. its; 23. fewer.

LESSON V

Page 104. Practice. 1. likely; 2. person; 3. really; 4. off; 5. many; 6. rarely; 7. have; 8. surely, slowly; 9. loose; 10. to; 11. likely, really; 12. from; 13. slowly; 14. lose; 15. Many; 16. really; 17. to; 18. slow; 19. have; 20. seldom; 21. person; 22. off; 23. likely; 24. really; 25. off; 26. loose, lose; 27. rarely; 28. surely; 29. have; 30. slowly.

LESSON VI

Page 105. Practice. 1. omit *there,* 2. omit *he,* 3. omit *had,* 4. omit *went and,* 5. omit *there;* 6. omit *a,* 7. omit *went and.*

REVIEW

Page 106. 1. affected; 2. into; 3. Many; 4. farther; 5. can; 6. from; 7. most adorable; 8. burst; 9. accept; 10. It's, its; 11. Behind; 12. enthusiastic; 13. as; 14. to; 15. all right; 16. very; 17. irritated; 18. fewer; 19. as; 20. strange; 21. an; 22. bad; 23. well; 24. slowly; 25. brother; 26. This; 27. except; 28. already; 29. anywhere; 30. as; 31. beside; 32. group; 33. have; 34. enthusiastic; 35. farther.

UNIT REVIEW

Page 107. 1. 2, 3; **2.** 1, 4; **3.** 1, 4; **4.** 1, 3; **5.** 2, 3; **6.** 2, 4; **7.** 1, 4; **8.** 1, 4; **9.** 1, 3; **10.** 1, 3; **11.** 2, 3; **12.** 1, 4; **13.** 2, 3.

UNIT 10: Vocabulary and Spelling
LESSON I: Synonyms

Page 108. Practice. absurd—foolish, silly; amateur—novice, beginner; awkward—clumsy, inept; comrade—friend, associate; concentrate—consolidate, strengthen; delay—wait, detain; demonstrate—show, exhibit; denied—contradicted, negated; eager—avid, enthusiastic; efficient—effective, capable; elevate—exalt, raise; essential—vital, necessary; feeble—decrepit, infirm; freedom—liberty, independence; gloomy—dark, murky; hide—conceal, secrete; indignant—angry, irate; interrogate—question, inquire of; interrupt—stop, hinder; pale—pallid, dim; prize—reward, trophy; shrewd—cunning, sagacious; visible—apparent, perceptible.

LESSON II: Antonyms

Page 109. Practice. 1. help—hinder; 2. cool—warm; 3. sold—bought; 4. dull—sharp; 5. clean—dirty; 6. lead—follow; 7. straight—crooked; 8. high—low; 9. lose—find; 10. admit—deny; 11. adversity—prosperity; 12. credit—debit; 13. advance—retreat; 14. vague—clear; 15. absent—present; 16. thrifty—wasteful; 17. stretch—shrink; 18. plentiful—scarce; 19. doubt—believe; 20. end—begin; 21. add—subtract; 22. free—confined; 23. good—evil; 24. rough—smooth; 25. spacious—cramped; 26. mean—kind; 27. pain—pleasure; 28. unique—common; 29. empty—full; 30. bitter—sweet; 31. dead—alive; 32. wide—narrow.

LESSON III: Homonyms and Spelling

Rules

Page 110. Practice 1. 1. week; 2. one, one, won; 3. fair, see, some, new; 4. sighed, plane, flew, sight; 5. claws, through, canvas; 6. deer, course; 7. heir, to, great;

Page 111. 8. site; 9. compliment, whose; 10. mail, route, due, it's; 11. shown, stationery; 12. bare, their, way, altar; 13. principal; 14. seam, seems; 15. plane, fare, fair. **Practice 2.** 1. a, 2. c, 3. b, 4. c, 5. c, 6. d, 7. a, 8. d, 9. b, 10. c, 11. b, 12. d,

Page 112. 13. b, 14. a. **Practice 3.** 1. moving, delayed; 2. boxes, lunches, beautifully; 3. replaying; 4. endorsement; 5. loaves; 6. losses, beginning.

Page 113. Practice 4. 1. Change *f* or *fe* to *v*, 2. if a word ends in a consonant preceded by a vowel, 3. when a consonant comes before the *y*, 4. when a word ends in —*y* preceded by a vowel, 5. when the suffix begins with a vowel.

Page 115. Practice 5. 1. a, 2. d, 3. d, 4. a, 5. a, 6. d, 7. c, 8. a, 9. a, 10. d, 11. a, 12. d, 13. b, 14. c, 15. d, 16. b, 17. d, 18. a, 19. c, 20. d, 21. d, 22. c, 23. c, 24. b, 25. a, 26. a, 27. a, 28. d, 29. c, 30. b, 31. b, 32. d, 33. a, 34. d.

UNIT REVIEW

Page 116. 1. 2, 3; **2.** 2, 3; **3.** 2, 4; **4.** 1, 4; **5.** 2, 3; **6.** 1, 4; **7.** 2, 3; **8.** 1, 3; **9.** 1, 3; **10.** 2, 4; **11.** 2, 3; **12.** 1, 4; **13.** 1, 4; **14.** 2, 3; **15.** 2, 4.

MASTERY TEST

Page 117. A. 1. 3, **2.** 4, **3.** 1. **B. 1.** 4, **2.** 5,
Page 118. 3. 4, **4.** 2, **5.** 3, **6.** 4, **7.** 3,
Page 119. 8. 5, **9.** 1, **10.** 2. **C. 1.** 2, 4; **2.** 1, 4; **3.** 1, 4; **4.** 1, 4; **5.** 2, 3; **6.** 2, 4; **7.** 2, 4; **8.** 2, 4;
Page 120. 9. 1, 4; **10.** 2, 3; **11.** 1, 3; **12.** 1, 4; **13.** 2, 3; **14.** 2, 4; **15.** 1, 3; **16.** 1, 4; **17.** 1, 4; **18.** 1, 3; **19.** 2, 3; **20.** 1, 4; **21.** 1, 3; **22.** 1, 3; **23.** 1, 4; **24.** 2, 4; **25.** 1, 4;
Page 121. 26. 1, 3; **27.** 2, 4; **28.** 1, 4; **29.** 2, 4; **30.** 1, 4; **31.** 2, 4; **32.** 2, 4; **33.** 1, 4; **34.** 1, 4; **35.** 1, 3; **36.** 2, 3; **37.** 1, 3; **38.** 1, 3; **39.** 2, 4; **40.** 1, 3; **41.** 2, 4; **42.** 2, 3;
Page 122. 43. 2, 4; **44.** 2, 4; **45.** 2, 4; **46.** 2, 3; **47.** 1, 4; **48.** 2, 3; **49.** 1, 3; **50.** 2, 4; **51.** 1, 4; **52.** 2, 4; **53.** 1, 4; **54.** 1, 4; **55.** 2, 3; **56.** 2, 4; **57.** 2, 3; **58.** 2, 3; **59.** 1, 3; **60.** 2, 4; **61.** 1, 4;
Page 123. 62. 2, 4; **63.** 2, 3; **64.** 2, 3; **65.** 2, 3; **66.** 1, 4; **67.** 2, 4; **68.** 2, 3; **69.** 1, 4; **70.** 2, 3; **71.** 1, 4; **72.** 1, 4; **73.** 2, 4; **74.** 1, 3. **D. 1.** "This painting," said Lupe, "will be auctioned next week." **2.** Jim, weren't you in New York on December 24, 1984? **3.** You should meet us within the hour, or we will be too late. **4.** After we change the oil in the car, we will shop for groceries. **5.** "That dog, an unusually friendly animal, belongs to Carlos," said Jean.